WRITTEN SKILLS FOR SQE

QUESTIONS & ANSWERS IN

BUSINESS LAW
AND PRACTICE

Sona Mehta

Series editors: Amy and David Sixsmith

REVISE
SQE

First published in 2024 by Fink Publishing Ltd

Impression number 10 9 8 7 6 5

British Library Cataloguing in Publication Data
A catalogue record for this book is available from the British Library
ISBN: 9781914213960

This book is also available in various ebook formats.
Ebook ISBN: 9781914213977

Cover and text design by BMLD (bmld.uk)
Production and typesetting by Westchester Publishing Services UK
Development editing by Llinos Edwards

Fink Publishing Ltd
E-mail: hello@revise4law.co.uk
www.revise4law.co.uk

Acknowledgements
The author and publisher would like to thank the following copyright holder for their kind permission to use material in this book:
RELX (UK) Limited, trading as LexisNexis: *Gore-Browne on Companies*, pp. 32 and 46; *Halsbury's Laws of England*, pp. 34 and 47; *Encyclopaedia of Forms and Precedents*, p. 44; *Tolley's Company Law Handbook*, p. 51.
Extracts from the SRA website in this book are owned by and published under licence from the Solicitors Regulation Authority of The Cube, 199 Wharfside Street, Birmingham, B1 1RN, which asserts its right to be identified as the author of this work in accordance with the Copyright, Designs and Patents Act 1988 Sections 77 and 78: www.sra.org.uk/solicitors/standards-regulations/financial-services-conduct-business-rules/. Please refer to the SRA website to ensure you are relying upon the correct version and most up to date version of the Standards.
Every effort has been made to obtain necessary permission with reference to copyright material. The publishers apologise if inadvertently any sources remain unacknowledged and will gladly make suitable arrangements with any copyright holders whom it has not been possible to contact.

Notes from the publisher
1. While Fink Publishing has made every attempt to ensure that advice on the qualification and its assessment is accurate, the official specification and associated assessment guidance materials are the only authoritative source of information and should always be referred to for definitive guidance. See the SRA website at https://sqe.sra.org.uk. Note that the SRA may amend their assessment guidance (including the contents of the assessment specifications) at any point.
2. Fink Publishing has robust editorial processes to ensure the accuracy of the content in this publication, and every effort is made to ensure this publication is free of errors. We are, however, only human, and occasionally errors do occur. Fink Publishing is not liable for any misunderstandings that arise as a result of errors in this publication, but it is our priority to ensure that the content is accurate. If you spot an error, please do contact us at **revise4law.co.uk** so we can make sure it is corrected.

Contents

Contributors   iv
Introduction   v

1   Case and matter analysis   1
    Question 1   2
        Sample answer 1 to question 1   6
        Sample answer 2 to question 1   9
    Question 2   11
        Sample answer 1 to question 2   14
        Sample answer 2 to question 2   17

2   Legal research   19
    Question 1   20
        Sample answer 1 to question 1   36
        Sample answer 2 to question 1   38
    Question 2   40
        Sample answer 1 to question 2   53
        Sample answer 2 to question 2   54

3   Legal writing   57
    Question 1   58
        Sample answer 1 to question 1   61
        Sample answer 2 to question 1   63
    Question 2   65
        Sample answer 1 to question 2   67
        Sample answer 2 to question 2   70

4   Legal drafting   73
    Question 1   75
        Sample answer 1 to question 1   79
        Sample answer 2 to question 1   82
    Question 2   85
        Sample answer 1 to question 2   88
        Sample answer 2 to question 2   91

Final words   94

Appendix   95
    Performance Indicators for SQE2 case and matter analysis
        assessment criteria   95
    Performance Indicators for SQE2 legal research assessment criteria   97
    Performance Indicators for SQE2 legal writing assessment criteria   99
    Performance Indicators for SQE2 legal drafting assessment criteria   101

Contributors

THE AUTHOR

Sona Mehta is an experienced senior lecturer who has been teaching the Legal Practice Course (LPC) at The City Law School, City, University of London, since 2006. She now teaches on the Solicitors' Practice Programme ('SPP'), the School's successor to the LPC, which is designed to prepare students for the SQE1 and SQE2 assessments as well as for a career as a solicitor. She has developed and co-ordinated modules on the skills of legal research, writing and drafting on the LPC and has taught business law and practice for many years. Sona has taught, developed and co-ordinated modules and assessments on the skills of legal research, writing and drafting in business law and practice for all of her academic career. Prior to teaching, Sona was a staff attorney at Blockbuster Entertainment Ltd where she was one of three in-house counsel providing general commercial legal advice and training to the business, having qualified and practised as a solicitor at Bird & Bird.

Sona is currently an external examiner for several universities, a senior fellow of Advance HE and an IAPP-certified information privacy professional/Europe and information privacy manager. She is also a keen advocate for developing opportunities for law students, running a mentoring scheme for her SPP students whilst being passionate about driving the EDI agenda.

SERIES EDITORS

Dr Amy Sixsmith is associate professor in law at the University of Sunderland and a senior fellow of Advance HE.

Dr David Sixsmith is assistant professor at Northumbria Law School and a senior fellow of Advance HE.

Introduction

Welcome to *Revise SQE: Legal Skills for SQE2*! This series of revision guides is designed to guide you through the second element of your Solicitors Qualifying Examination, in which you will be tested on your ability to put the legal knowledge you acquired for your SQE1 assessment into six different practical contexts.

The key to successfully navigating your SQE2 assessment can be split into three distinct areas:
• understanding how you are being assessed and what you are being assessed on
• practising example scenarios
• comparing and contrasting your answers with sample answers.

Our SQE2 guides are here to help you with this process, providing you not only with helpful guidance and top tips for approaching all of the relevant skills, but also with multiple sample questions for each assessable skill in each of the relevant legal disciplines. Samples of high and lower scoring threshold answers to each question are provided to guide you in good practice – and steer you away from potential pitfalls.

Using this series in conjunction with our series of SQE1 revision guides, to ensure that your legal knowledge is accurate and up to date, will enable you to tackle your SQE2 assessment with confidence.

PREPARING YOURSELF FOR SQE

The SQE is the route to qualification for aspiring solicitors and consists of two parts, as shown in this table.

Assessment	Contents of assessment
SQE1	• 360 multiple-choice questions • Closed book • Assessed over 2 sittings • Over 10 hours in total
SQE2	• Practical legal skills • 16 written and oral assessments • Assesses 6 practical legal skills • Over 14 hours in total

In addition to the above assessments all candidates will have to undertake two years' qualifying work experience. More information on the SQE assessments can be found on the SRA website.

It is important to note that the SQE can be perceived to be a 'harder' set of assessments than the Legal Practice Course (LPC). The reason for this, explained by the SRA, is that the LPC is designed to prepare candidates for 'day one' of their training contract; the SQE, on the other hand, is designed to prepare candidates for 'day one' of being a newly qualified solicitor. With that in mind, and a different style of assessments in place, it is understandable that you might feel nervous or wary of the SQE.

This revision guide series will focus on preparation for SQE2. The SQE2 assessment is challenging as it asks candidates to put into practice the knowledge that they acquired for SQE1. This style of assessment is likely to be different from what you will have experienced before. In this Introduction and revision guide series, we hope to alleviate some of those concerns, with guidance on preparing for the SQE assessment, tips on how to approach the skills-based assessments and detailed commentaries on sample answers to aid your revision.

WHAT DOES SQE2 ENTAIL?

SQE2 is split into two parts: oral and written. The table below shows the contexts in which these skills are assessed.

Part	Skills	Contexts
Oral	Client interview and attendance note / legal analysis (hereafter referred to as 'interviewing')	Property practice Wills and intestacy, probate administration and practice
	Advocacy	Dispute resolution Criminal litigation
Written	Case and matter analysis Legal research Legal writing Legal drafting	Criminal litigation Dispute resolution Property practice Wills and intestacy, probate administration and practice Business organisations, rules and procedures

Oral skills

You will sit four oral skills examinations, which will take place over two half-days.

On day one you will be assessed in:
• advocacy in the context of dispute resolution
• interviewing in the context of property practice.

On day two you will be assessed in:
• advocacy in the context of criminal litigation
• interviewing in the context of wills and intestacy, probate administration and practice.

Written skills

For the written skills assessment, you will sit 12 examinations that will take place over three half-days. Every day you will be required to take an assessment in *each* of the written skills – legal research, case and matter analysis, legal writing and legal drafting.

On day one you will sit:
- two assessments in dispute resolution
- two assessments in criminal litigation.

On day two you will sit:
- two assessments in property practice
- two assessments in wills and intestacy, probate administration and practice.

On day three you will sit all four assessments in business organisations, rules and procedures.

HOW IS SQE2 MARKED?

Each of the SQE2 skills has its own set of assessment criteria. The *Revise SQE: Legal Skills for SQE2* series will include the following:
- Oral skills – the criteria are outlined in **Oral Skills for SQE2: Client Interviewing and Negotiation** and **Oral Skills for SQE2: Advocacy**.
- Written skills – the criteria are outlined at the beginning of each chapter in our books covering the written skills for different legal contexts (see pages 2, 20, 58 and 74 in this text).

The assessment is marked against the relevant criteria using the following scale:
A. Superior performance: well above the competency requirements of the assessment.
B. Clearly satisfactory: clearly meets the competency requirements of the assessment.
C. Marginal pass: on balance, just meets the competency requirements of the assessment.
D. Marginal fail: on balance, just fails to meet the competency requirements of the assessment.
E. Clearly unsatisfactory: clearly does not meet the competency requirements of the assessment.
F. Poor performance: well below the competency requirements of the assessment.

Your mark will be calculated by converting the grade into a numerical mark, with A representing 5 marks and F representing 0 marks.

The scaled scoring system

In January 2025 the SRA introduced a scaled scoring system for all SQE2 assessments. This approach is designed to ensure that candidate scores are comparable across different assessment sittings, thereby providing a fair and consistent measure of candidate performance. The same system has already been implemented for all SQE1 assessments.

The scaled scoring system works in the following way:
- Initially, candidates will receive a 'raw score' based on their performance across the 16 assessment stations in SQE2.
- A pass mark is then set for each assessment window. The pass mark is determined using statistical methods that account for any differences in question difficulty. This ensures fairness across different exam versions.
- Candidate raw scores are then converted to a common scale ranging from 0 to 500, with the pass mark consistently set at 300. This standardisation allows for direct comparisons between candidates' performances, regardless of the specific assessments they completed.

When you access your results, you will be able to see:
- a detailed breakdown of your results by assessment station (results will be expressed as marks from 0 to 5 for each assessment criterion across each of the 16 assessment stations)
- your overall mark expressed as a percentage
- your scaled score out of 500 – remember that the pass mark will always be set at 300.

For more information about the scaled scoring system, visit https://sqe.sra.org.uk/SQEHomePage.

It is very important that you are aware of the standard you are required to meet. The competence standard is that of a Day One Solicitor, which is mapped against Level 3 of the Threshold Standard for the Statement of Solicitor Competence. This is available on the SRA website, and we would encourage you to review this prior to sitting your SQE2 assessment.

The assessors

In terms of who will be assessing you against this standard, and the relevant skills criteria, the interview will be marked by the person you are interviewing, while the remaining assessments (attendance note, advocacy and all written skills) will be marked by a solicitor. All assessors will have received training on how to assess a candidate's performance against the relevant criteria. It is therefore essential that you tackle your assessments in the same way that you would if you were a fully qualified solicitor on the first day of practice – with professionalism, confidence and calmness. This will come across to the assessors in the examination itself: remember that they are fundamentally assessing your suitability for practice!

WHERE DOES *REVISE SQE* COME INTO IT?

This new series of revision guides for SQE2 will provide you with helpful tips and advice on how to tackle each skill assessment in the relevant contexts. Each book provides a range of example threshold answers to SQE2-style assessment questions, which you can use to practise and assess your answers against, to see how you are performing in each individual area. This is designed to assist with your revision and consolidate your understanding of how key topics could be assessed in the SQE2 examination. We hope that this series will give clarity for the assessment focus, provide useful tips for sitting SQE2 and also act as a general revision aid.

Finally, always keep in mind that while SQE2 is primarily a skills-based assessment, you are still being tested on your knowledge of the law. It is therefore important that you conduct an honest self-evaluation on the areas of the SQE1 specification with which you feel you need further support. *Revise SQE* can help you with this:
- Check out the 'SQE1 Revision Checklist' for each of our SQE1 revision guides on our website: **www.revise4law.co.uk**. These will help you to identify which substantive topics you feel confident about being assessed on, and which ones you need to revise.
- All of our *Revise SQE* revision guides are mapped to the relevant SRA specifications. Before taking the SQE2 assessments, remember to look back at our revision guides for SQE1 if you have any gaps in your legal knowledge.

1

Case and matter analysis

■ MAKE SURE YOU KNOW

This chapter deals with the skill of case and matter analysis in the context of business organisations, rules and procedures. Case and matter analysis in this area is one of the skills that will be assessed on day three of the SQE2 Written Skills assessments (see the Introduction for more detail). The SQE2 can test candidates' knowledge of the legal principles and practices associated with business organisations, business taxation, money laundering and financial services. Remember, business organisations are commercial enterprises that generally operate for generating a profit. So, when advising a client it is important to consider the commercial consequence of any action you propose a business to take, in addition to the legal impact.

We advise that you read this SQE2 revision guide once you are familiar with the contents of **Revise SQE: Business Law and Practice**. This chapter provides examples of how different scenarios relating to business organisations, rules and procedures, taxation, money laundering and financial services could arise in the context of an SQE2 case and matter analysis assessment.

■ SQE ASSESSMENT ADVICE

As you work through this chapter, remember to pay particular attention in your revision to:
- the inclusion of relevant facts in the sample answers
- the way in which the advice given is tailored to the client/recipient and the information you are given about them in the sample assessments
- how the stronger sample answers use clear and concise language
- how the law is applied to the client's situation
- the way in which any ethical or professional conduct issues are identified and resolved.

See the Appendix for the SRA's performance indicators in case and matter analysis.

■ INTRODUCTION TO CASE AND MATTER ANALYSIS IN BUSINESS ORGANISATIONS, RULES AND PROCEDURES

It is likely that your SQE2 assessment will replicate scenarios which occur in day-to-day legal practice. As with all disciplines, a key aspect of practising in the field of business organisations, rules and procedures is the ability to follow up advice given by a solicitor to a client over the telephone or at a meeting with a clearly articulated written communication. Your SQE2 case and matter analysis assessment will be based on reading a memorandum or email from a partner which asks you to provide advice to a client. This will usually follow a fictitious telephone call which has taken place between the partner and the client. While the question itself will give you some direction about the areas you need to cover in your letter or email, you will be required to apply your knowledge of those areas to the scenario and communicate the relevant advice to the client, clearly and concisely, in writing. This chapter will provide examples of how you can do this and meet the criteria for the SQE2 case and matter analysis assessment at the same time.

The key to success in your SQE2 case and matter analysis assessment is approaching the question in a structured manner. Try adopting the following approach:

1. Once you have read the question, write down the key legal and procedural points.
2. Identify what you think the client wants to achieve, not just from a legal perspective.
3. Consider which of points 1 and 2 above you feel needs to be communicated to the client.
4. Write your answer.
5. Review your answer, keeping in mind the SQE2 case and matter analysis assessment criteria.

Assessment technique

When reviewing your answer, make sure everything in your letter is relevant to answering the client's question. This technique stops you from addressing tangential points that the client has not asked about.

SQE2 case and matter analysis assessment criteria

Try to remember these points as you construct your answer:

Skills

1. Identify relevant facts.
2. Provide client-focused advice (ie advice which demonstrates an understanding of the problem from the client's point of view and what the client wants to achieve, not just from a legal perspective).
3. Use clear, precise, concise and acceptable language.

Application of law

4. Apply the law correctly to the client's situation.
5. Apply the law comprehensively to the client's situation, identifying any ethical and professional conduct issues and exercising judgement to resolve them honestly and with integrity.

In chapter 1 of **Revise SQE: Business Law and Practice**, we considered the different options for forming a business. Question 1 below demonstrates how your knowledge of this topic could be tested in the context and format of an SQE2 case and matter analysis assessment.

■ QUESTION 1

Email to candidate

From: Partner
Sent: 10 January 202#
To: Candidate
Subject: Business Development – Wested Candies

I recently met Westin John, an entrepreneurial friend of my son who is looking to start a new business selling high-end cocktail-flavoured sweets. I sampled a few of the candies and I was extremely impressed! Westin has been working with his friend Edwina Bonney in creating the product – Westin being responsible for the flavour and Edwina the packaging. They are both living at home with their respective parents. The pair have up until now been making the sweets as gifts for friends' parties, but have received lots of enquiries and are now seriously considering expanding their enterprise.

The proposal
Westin has savings of £5,000 that he is prepared to invest in the business. Edwina has £500. The pair have agreed that any profits would be split between them according to their initial investment, so Westin would receive 90%, Edwina 10%. Westin anticipates all decisions being made by mutual agreement. They want to call the business 'Wested Candies'.

The pair want to focus on building up the business and gaining a competitive advantage, and don't want to give anyone the opportunity to explore how they operate and what their accounts look like – certainly during the initial development phase of the business.

Edwina thinks that they should set up in partnership and has sent Westin the attached email (Attachment 1) and draft Partnership Agreement (Attachment 2) which he has forwarded to me.

Background
Westin is very familiar with corporate structures and the regulatory requirements for companies; he is director of a small start-up company in which he owns shares. However, he is less familiar with partnerships. He believes there are fewer formalities for partnerships and that partners have more personal liability than directors; but would like more clarification of the position. I promised to send him a summary of how a partnership operates and the liabilities of partners.

Advice and analysis required
Westin would like advice about this partnership proposal, the privacy afforded to partnerships, and the responsibilities and liabilities of partners. He would also like to know how he could minimise his liability.

Please prepare a memorandum to me providing this advice and analysis to use as the basis for a letter to Westin. In providing this advice, please bear in mind that Westin has no experience in operating a partnership.

Please set out your advice and analysis on the following:

1. **If Wested Candies was set up as a partnership, what reporting and disclosure requirements would exist, and what would Westin's and Edwina's liabilities and responsibilities be as partners?**
2. **What additional provisions would you include in the Partnership Agreement to minimise Westin's liability? You should suggest proposals that will benefit Westin, keeping in mind what you think might be acceptable to Edwina, and explain why you would include them.**

Thanks

Partner

Attachment 1

From: edwina.bonney@email.com
To: Westinjohn@blahoo.com
Subject: Wested Candies

Westin, hi
I'm so excited to develop the business!
I've done some digging around and think the best way for us to proceed is to start up as a partnership – there seem to be no rules that we need to comply with, no reporting or disclosure requirements either. It looks like we can keep the whole venture under wraps as a partnership with no need to file accounts or anything!

I'm happy with a 90/10 split in your favour – you are the engineer, after all!

I've attached a Partnership Agreement that I think could work – I don't really think we need much else, but do let me know what you think. I suppose we should have something formalised.

Speak soon

Ed

Attachment 2

Partnership Agreement between:
(1) **Edwina Bonney** of 53 Rose Gardens, Hampstead, London NW3 4JT (**'Edwina'**) and
(2) **Westin John** of 8 The Spinney, River Road, London W6 2ET (**'Westin'**)

BACKGROUND
(A) Edwina and Westin (the **'Partners'**) want to carry on the business of making and selling cocktail-flavoured sweets (**'Partnership Business'**).
(B) The Partners want to carry on the Partnership Business under the terms of this agreement.

Commencement and duration
1. The Partnership Business shall commence on [   ] and continue until it is terminated.

Name
2. The Partnership Business shall operate under the name Wested Candies.
Capital
3. On the date of this agreement, each partner shall contribute capital to the partnership carried on by the Partners for the purpose of the Partnership Business (**'Partnership'**) as follows:
    a. Westin shall contribute £5,000
    b. Edwina shall contribute £500.

Partnership property
4. Any assets (or rights in them) which are used by the Partnership for the purposes of the Partnership Business shall belong to the Partners in the proportions in which they contributed to share in capital.

Profits and losses
5. The profits and losses of the Partnership shall belong to and be borne by the Partners in proportion to their capital contribution as set out in Clause 3 above.

* * *

■ YOUR TURN

Have a go at answering question 1, remembering the guidance on pages 1–2.
- Refer to the structured approach in the SRA's assessment criteria on page 2.
- Create a list of the most salient legal points raised by the question.
- Consider the client's perspective at all times.
- Timings are important: you will need to prepare and write your answer in one hour.

SQE1 Functioning legal knowledge link
Remember from chapters 1 and 2 of **Revise SQE: Business Law and Practice** that no formalities are required to set up a partnership, and a partnership agreement is not a strict requirement. There are some clear benefits to having a partnership agreement, including providing clarity and customisation to suit the client's intentions.

EVALUATING YOUR ANSWER

When you have attempted question 1, mark it yourself against the SQE2 case and matter analysis assessment criteria. Do you think your attempt met the threshold standard?

Now compare your attempt with the following key legal points and two sample answers to question 1. A circled number indicates that commentary is provided for this part of the answer. The commentary will explain whether or not the sample is likely to meet the threshold SQE2 standard.

➡Key legal points: Question 1

Note, PA 1890 refers to the Partnership Act 1890.

- A partnership has no separate legal personality, so cannot own assets or incur a liability as a separate legal entity. Partners hold assets and incur liability on behalf of a partnership.
- There are no public reporting or disclosure requirements for partnerships, but partnerships of 20 people or fewer must state the names of each of the partners and an address in the United Kingdom for service of documents on all business letters, written orders for goods, invoices, receipts and written demands for payment.
- Partnerships should keep their own accounts, which can remain private and do not need to be audited. Partners must include information about their income/loss from a partnership in their own personal tax calculations.
- Partners must render true accounts and full information in matters affecting the partnership to any partner (s 28 PA 1890).
- Partners do not have to adopt formal 'roles' in a partnership. Section 24 PA 1890 sets out some provisions relating to the rights and obligations of partners, but these can be varied by contrary agreement. For example, partners have the right to be involved in the management of the business (s 24(5) PA 1890) and the firm should indemnify every partner in respect of payments made, and liabilities incurred by them, in the course of the firm's business (s 24(2) PA 1890).
- Partners owe each other fiduciary duties, such as a duty of the utmost good faith and account for all profits made by them from carrying on any business of the same nature as, and competing with, that of the firm, without the consent of the other partners.
- Partners are jointly liable for the contractual debts of a partnership (s 9 PA 1890).
- Wrongful acts or omissions, such as torts, of any partner acting in the ordinary course of the business or with the authority of the other partners gives rise to joint and several liability.

- Some key matters to address in a partnership agreement could include:
  - capital profit share
  - entitlement to interest on capital
  - partnership property
  - decision making
  - indemnity from each partner to the other
  - limiting an individual partner's ability to commit the partnership.

■ SAMPLE ANSWER 1 TO QUESTION 1

Memorandum

Westin John wants to set up a business with Edwina Bonney making and selling cocktail-flavoured sweets. Westin develops the flavours and makes the sweets, while Edwina packages them. This enterprise began as a hobby but is gaining traction and the pair are considering how to formalise this business. Both individuals are keen to preserve the confidentiality of the organisation and not be subjected to unnecessary regulation, so feel setting up a partnership called Wested Candies to be the preferred option. Edwina has provided a draft Partnership Agreement. Westin is unfamiliar with how partnerships operate and the extent of a partner's liability, and would like some advice on this and the draft Agreement. **❶**

1. Reporting and disclosure requirements for a partnership **❷**

There are no reporting or disclosure requirements for a partnership, except in relation to:

  a. information about the names of the partners and address for service being available on stationery; and
  b. information about the identity of the partners being made available to HMRC.

Consequently, if Wested Candies was set up as a partnership, its accounts and business affairs would remain private and free from regulation.

Separate accounts should be kept for the partnership's operations, but as partnerships are not separate legal entities, each partner would have to include any profits/losses from the partnership in their own personal tax calculations.

2. Liabilities and responsibilities for partners of Wested Candies **❸**

Liabilities

Partners are jointly and severally liable for debts incurred by a partner who acts in the ordinary course of business of the partnership. This liability is uncapped. So, a judgment could be obtained against Wested Candies and could be enforced against the assets of the partnership. If these were insufficient to cover the judgment, the judgment could be enforced against assets owned by either Westin or Edwina, or both of them.

Westin appears to have significantly more savings available than Edwina. If he has more assets available than Edwina, creditors may opt to pursue him rather than Edwina for any outstanding partnership debts. Westin would be liable to pay these from his personal funds. He might then be able to recover the funds from Edwina, if this was expressly agreed between them in the partnership agreement. **④**

Responsibilities

Partners do not have to adopt formal 'roles' in a partnership. Where there is no agreement, they have the right to be involved in the management of the partnership, but there is no obligation for a partner to exercise this right. Partners have a responsibility for sharing any losses made by the business unless the partners expressly agree otherwise.

Partners owe their fellow partners fiduciary duties such as:

- a duty of the utmost good faith; and
- a duty to account for all profits made by them from carrying on any business of the same nature as and competing with that of the firm, without the consent of the other partners.

These fiduciary duties cannot be varied or disclaimed.

3. Additional provisions to the partnership agreement ⑤

While a partnership can exist without a formal agreement, it is always advisable for partners to have a written agreement clearly setting out the terms agreed, rather than leaving these issues to be resolved by the default provisions in section 24 of the Partnership Act 1890 and the court.

I have set out below some key provisions that I would recommend be added to the draft document forwarded by Edwina.

To minimise Westin's liability

a. Limit the authority of one partner alone to commit Wested Candies

One partner should only be able to act alone to commit the partnership to small contracts, for example, those of £1,000 or less. That way, both Westin and Edwina would need to sign off on all larger commitments binding the partnership. Any third parties dealing with the partnership should also be made aware of such restriction – for example by including a footer at the end of all emails stating any commitments to bind the partnership for an amount over £1,000 will only be valid if signed by both parties. This would mean that if a contract is entered into in breach of this restriction, Wested Candies as a partnership would not be liable.

b. Indemnify the other partner

Westin and Edwina should indemnify each other for all losses incurred by one partner if that partner acted in accordance with the agreement. For example, if Westin was sued for a partnership debt and subsequently paid it, Edwina should indemnify him against the losses he incurred so that Westin alone would not bear the burden. However, an indemnity here would only be of benefit if Edwina had the financial means to reimburse Westin. Westin should make enquiries into Edwina's financial status to be aware of her position. ⑥

To address the operation of the partnership ⑦

The draft Partnership Agreement does not address some operational issues relating to the partnership such as:

- how decisions should be made and whether one partner alone can commit Wested Candies
- how much time each partner must devote to the business
- whether capital profits should be split differently from income profits
- how any property/assets used for partnership should be owned
- what should happen if either Westin or Edwina wanted to leave the partnership.

While there is legislation and case law considering some of these matters, it would be sensible to address any issues that can be anticipated, such as those set out above, clearly in the Agreement rather than leave it to the courts to determine. Please let me know if this is something you would like me to prepare.

COMMENTARY

1 The introductory paragraph sets out the relevant facts and the purpose of the memorandum. It is important to establish clearly from the outset exactly what the relevant facts are and what the client is seeking advice on, and to maintain that client-focused approach throughout the memorandum.

2 In the section entitled '**Reporting and disclosure requirements for a partnership**', note how the heading for this section uses the express wording from the question posed by the partner. This lets the examiner know that the candidate is focused on addressing the client's concerns, which is one of the criteria against which they are being assessed. The text then sets out brief details of the reporting and disclosure requirements relating to the partners' names and an address for service of documents and HMRC. It does not elaborate on these requirements in great detail, but merely provides a very brief summary.

3 Throughout the memorandum, the use of headings assists in providing clear, precise advice and a logical, coherent structure. In addition, the law is set out and then applied to the client's situation, referring to Westin, Edwina and 'Wested Candies' instead of the generic, impersonal terms 'partners' and the 'partnership'.

4 The section entitled '**Liabilities and responsibilities for partners of Wested Candies**' begins by setting out the liabilities for partners. One of the critical aspects of liability of partners is that relating to joint liability. This is elaborated upon using the names of the client (Westin) and his proposed partner (Edwina). This is a good technique to show the examiner that the candidate understands the client's situation and is applying the relevant law or principles to that situation.

5 The section entitled '**Additional provisions to the partnership agreement**' is then split into two different headings and subheadings (minimising Westin's liability and addressing the operation of the partnership) to provide some structure to the final paragraphs.

6 A solution is set out, and then an explanation provided as to why it is necessary/ appropriate. Practical and commercial advice relating to the financial resources available to the indemnifier is given; this is a good example of providing client-focused comprehensive advice not just from a legal perspective.

7 This section contains examples of additional provisions that could be inserted into the Agreement for clarity and to minimise Westin's liability, with a brief explanation as to why. By using examples, this again demonstrates how the provisions might work to secure Westin's position.

Does this answer meet the threshold?

The sample answer above sets out clear, precise and concise advice relating to the client's concerns. It addresses the reporting and disclosure requirements that exist for a partnership, and what Westin's and Edwina's liabilities and responsibilities would be as partners. It also provides some suggested additional provisions for inclusion in the Partnership Agreement to benefit the client, with an explanation as to why they might be of benefit to Westin, ensuring the advice is client-focused. It is therefore likely to meet the threshold standard for the SQE2 case and matter analysis assessment.

Note how each of the assessment criteria for case and matter analysis are dealt with and in the appropriate place, where the examiner is directed specifically to the areas of the report which deal with those criteria. It is important to remember that this is an assessment after all: let your examiners know that you are familiar with the criteria by which you are being assessed!

Now consider the second sample answer to question 1.

■ SAMPLE ANSWER 2 TO QUESTION 1

Memorandum

Thank you for requesting that I deal with this query regarding partnerships. ❶

I am happy to confirm that there are no reporting or disclosure obligations or requirements for partnerships. Westin and Eddie ❷ will not need to worry about filings once a partnership is established. ❸ A partner can keep their business affairs and accounts private and confidential as there is no filing obligation, nor a register that the public can access and interrogate for partnerships. ❹ Furthermore, there are no specific roles partners must undertake. Partners are, however, liable for the debts of the partnership. ❺ The extent of a partner's liability would depend on the type of authority they had for acting on behalf of the partnership. Partners can act with actual or apparent authority. ❻

As for responsibilities, partners owe fiduciary duties to one another. There are three of these set out in the Partnership Act 1890: s 28 – the duty to provide true accounts and full information on partnership matters; s 29 – the duty to account for profits derived from the position as a partner; and s 30 – the duty to account for profits from a competing business. ❼

A partnership can exist without a written agreement. Indeed, there are many partnerships that do, as they benefit from the privacy and lack of disclosure as referred to above. The provisions of the Partnership Act 1890, particularly those in s 24, provide a wide range of default terms for the arrangement between the partners which would be more than adequate for the needs of Westin and Eddie. ❽

Finally, Westin could, if he really wanted to, minimise his liability by inserting the following clause:

> Any contracts entered into on behalf of Wested Candies will only be valid and binding if signed by Westin John. ❾

I hope the above is helpful. Please let me know how you would like me to proceed.

COMMENTARY

❶ This memorandum fails to begin by setting out the relevant facts. It is important to establish what the client wants to know and then identify information that is relevant to answering their questions.

❷ The two business partners are Westin and Edwina. The instructions did not refer to 'Eddie', so including this reference in the memorandum is utilising a fact that is incorrect.

❸ You are required to apply the law correctly and comprehensively to the client's situation. While partnerships do not need to submit filings to Companies House, each partner is responsible for their own income tax, and profits from a partnership will be included in an individual partner's income tax calculation. This should be flagged up to the client, as it would be an example of demonstrating an understanding of the issues from the client's point of view addressing not just legal issues; therefore stating that they 'will not need to worry about filings once a partnership is established' is not entirely correct. The candidate should set out what the comprehensive legal position is (that there is no formal record-keeping obligation), how it would affect the client (the client must incorporate his share of the partnership's profit/loss into his own personal tax calculation) and the consequences of this (that partnership accounts should be maintained).

④ Note the language of this sentence. It is not precise nor concise, but instead unnecessarily wordy, which does not meet the assessment criteria.

⑤ While the memorandum does correctly state that partners are liable for the debts of the partnership, this statement should be elaborated upon. No reference is made to this liability being unlimited. This is a very important aspect of partnerships and should be stressed to the client, particularly as this is a key difference compared to companies. Including this information would be an example of demonstrating an understanding of the problem from the client's perspective.

⑥ As stated above, it is important to provide client-focused advice. These sentences are correct, but they state legal principles without providing a context for the client, so do not provide client-focused advice. A client might not appreciate the distinction between actual or apparent authority – and the use of such terminology without an explanation is likely to be penalised in an assessment.

⑦ The term 'fiduciary duties' is introduced without an explanation of what this means. This is not client-friendly and does not assist with the provision of client-focused advice. In addition, the language is not clear for a client. This paragraph then goes on to summarise the provisions of three sections of the Partnership Act. The summaries are not client-focused nor explained from the client's point of view.

⑧ This paragraph does not really provide comprehensive advice. The instructions were to provide a memorandum that could then be used in a letter to the client. If the memorandum were to be sent to the client, it would not be appropriate to refer to s 24 Partnership Act as it introduces unnecessary technical terms. Also, it is well established that s 24 Partnership Act is not comprehensive in addressing the terms of a partnership agreement, so stating that it would be more than adequate for the client is a failure to apply the law correctly to the client's situation.

⑨ This sentence does provide some draft wording for insertion into the Partnership Agreement, but there is no explanation as to why this might minimise Westin's liability.

Does this answer meet the threshold?

When assessing the second letter against the SQE2 case and matter analysis assessment criteria, it is unlikely that this memorandum would meet the threshold standard for the assessment. The advice provided refers to concepts such as 'fiduciary duty' and sections of the Partnership Act without adequate explanation, resulting in the letter not providing client-focused advice. The memorandum answer does not demonstrate an understanding of the problem from the client's perspective.

As you know, SQE2 can assess any of the areas on the SQE1 Business Law and Practice specification. Below is another example of how a different part of the specification (insolvency) could arise in the context of case and matter analysis in the context of business organisations, rules and procedures on SQE2.

■ QUESTION 2

Email to candidate

From: Partner
Sent: 1 February 202#
To: Candidate
Subject: Jim's Gems Ltd

I met Jim Pope, Managing Director of Jim's Gems Ltd ('JGL') yesterday. JGL is a company that sells coloured stones to people who make their own jewellery. We helped set the firm up about ten years ago. It sells mainly to individuals who make jewellery as a hobby. I have attached a Company Search Report that was done yesterday (Attachment 1).

Up until last year, business was flourishing and JGL expanded its range of products to include beads to appeal to a younger audience. The company spent £40,000 on online marketing campaigns last year, timed to coincide with both the Christmas and summer school holidays. This drive brought in a lot of new business which more than covered the cost of the marketing.

Unfortunately, JGL's supplier of blue beads stopped trading earlier this year and the company sourced a new supplier, Aqua Stones Ltd ('ASL'). ASL provided cheaper beads of all colours, and JGL switched beads supplier to ASL. The transition to ASL seemed seamless until a customer complained about the colour of the beads rubbing off on their fingers. Complaints then started rushing in via social media and JGL's customer review rating has plummeted. As a result, JGL has lost many of its loyal customers very quickly and is now struggling to generate business.

Storage costs and overheads are increasing, and Jim thinks the company will struggle to pay its bills in the next few months. In particular, Jim is concerned about the following invoices that are due in the coming weeks:

- £7,500 for the next delivery of gems from another supplier
- £2,000 loan repayment to Westminster Bank
- £500 for the courier costs.

JGL also borrowed £3,000 from Stewart Chan, the nephew of its Finance Director, Fifi Li, a few months ago. The loan is repayable over a three-year term, at an interest rate of 5%. Stewart is getting married next year and Fifi has proposed to the other directors that this loan is repaid as soon as possible.

JGL's production director, Ashwin Shah has procured an offer from Bling Ltd of £9,000 for some of JGL's red and green stones that are currently in storage (Attachment 2). The current market value of those stones is £40,000. Fifi does not think this is a reasonable offer for the stones.

Advice and analysis required

Jim would like advice about: payment of the invoices; the offer from Bling of £9,000 for the stones; and the liability of him and the other directors.

I would like you to provide this advice and analysis for me to use as a basis of a letter to advise the client company. In providing your advice, please bear in mind that Jim has no experience of managing a company in financial difficulties.

Please ensure that you include brief explanations of the relevant law where appropriate.

Please set out your advice and analysis on the following:

1. **Is JGL obliged to accept Bling's offer for the stones and use the funds to pay its suppliers, bank and courier costs (in that order?) Is there any alternative or additional action you would advise JGL to take?**
2. **Could the directors of the company be personally liable for any of the company's debts? Could they avoid this?**

Thanks

Partner

Note to candidates:

You can assume that all professional conduct and client matters have been dealt with.

Attachment 1

COMPANY SEARCH REPORT

Company name:	Jim's Gems Ltd ('JGL')
Company number:	9202733
Issued share capital:	100,000 ordinary shares of £1 each (fully paid)
Articles:	Model articles without amendment
Registered office:	23 Littleton Place, London W1 3BB
Charges:	Westminster Bank – First fixed charge over all JGL's assets up to £250,000 (Duly registered at Companies House on 01.02.2020)
Liquidators/Receivers	None appointed
Company secretary	Fifi Li
Directors:	Jim Pope – managing director and chair Fifi Li – finance director Ashwin Shah – production director
Shareholders	Jim Pope – 50,000 ordinary shares Fifi Li – 25,000 ordinary shares Ashwin Shah – 10,000 ordinary shares Hussain Abbas – 15,000 ordinary shares

Attachment 2

Bling Ltd
Glitzy House
Creedy Street
Birmingham
B3 9LT

Ashwin Shah
Jim's Gems Ltd
23 Littleton Place
London W1 3BB

20 January 202#

Dear Ashwin,

I refer to our recent telephone conversation. As I mentioned, Bling Ltd is in the business of selling coloured rocks and stones, but currently has a shortage of red and green items.

You mentioned that you may have some to spare.

We'd like to offer to buy:

> 1500 x 60 kg bags of red stones; and
> 1500 x 60 kg bags of green stones

For a sum of £9,000 incl of VAT and delivery.

This offer is only valid for 30 days from receipt of this letter.

Please call me if you are interested in this offer.

Yours sincerely

Randolph Stobbard

Bling Ltd

* * *

■ YOUR TURN

Have a go at answering question 2, remembering the guidance on pages 1-2.
* Refer to the structured approach in the SRA's assessment criteria on page 2.
* Create a list of the most salient legal points raised by the question.
* Consider the client's perspective at all times.
* Timings are important: you will need to prepare and write your answer in one hour.

SQE1 Functioning legal knowledge link
Remember from chapter 6 of *Revise SQE: Business Law and Practice* that an insolvent company may go into liquidation. A liquidator takes over the control of the company and the directors' powers cease. The liquidator has powers to investigate and unwind past transactions, where permitted under the Insolvency Act 1986. Directors owe duties to a company, but remember that a director of an insolvent company may be liable to contribute to the assets of a company where the company continued to trade, and they knew or ought to have concluded that there was no reasonable prospect of the company avoiding insolvency proceedings.

EVALUATING YOUR ANSWER

When you have attempted question 2, mark it yourself against the SQE2 case and matter analysis assessment criteria. Do you think your attempt met the threshold standard?

Now compare your attempt with the following key legal points and the two sample answers to question 2. A circled number indicates that commentary is provided for this part of the answer. The commentary explains whether or not the sample satisfies the assessment criteria, and accordingly likely to meet the threshold SQE2 standard.

➡️Key legal points: Question 2

* There are several situations in which a company is deemed to be insolvent as set out in s 123 Insolvency Act 1986.
* One of those grounds is if it can be proved to the court that the company cannot pay its debts as they fall due (often known as the 'cash flow test') – s 123(1)(e).
* If a company is deemed to be insolvent, a liquidator could be appointed to collect the company's assets and review past transactions (including transactions at an undervalue and voidable preferences).

- If either a transaction at an undervalue or a voidable preference is proved, the transaction will be voidable at the court's discretion and the property might be returned to the company.
- The directors of a company that is or may be insolvent must take all steps they can to remedy the situation, with particular reference to s 172(3) Companies Act 2006.
- If directors do not take all such steps, they may be personally liable on liquidation or administration.
- Some steps the directors could take include:
  - putting the company into liquidation
  - negotiating extended payment terms with the creditors
  - entering into company voluntary arrangements with the creditors
  - appointing an administrator to run the company and sell it as a going concern
  - utilising the moratorium procedure
  - entering into a restructuring plan or scheme of arrangement.

■ SAMPLE ANSWER 1 TO QUESTION 2

Jim's Gems has been trading quite successfully for many years until recently when it received negative reviews which resulted in a significant loss of business. The company is now experiencing cash flow issues and there are concerns that it will be unable to pay its upcoming invoices. I have set out below a summary of the options available to the company and the liability implications for directors. ❶

Summary of liquidation process ❷

Where a company is unable to pay its debts as they fall due, a creditor might submit a petition to the court for the company to be shut down – effectively go into liquidation. As you have indicated that Jim's Gems may struggle to pay its bills over the coming months, this could be a very real prospect for the company.

If the liquidation petition is served and order granted, a liquidator will be appointed to take control of Jim's Gems. The liquidator's role would then be to gather as much of the company's assets as it can, to sell them off in order to pay the creditors in an order that is prescribed by law. The liquidator can investigate certain past transactions and potentially apply to the court to have these set aside. Assets might then be returned to the company for the liquidator to dispose of to repay the creditors, and the directors might also be held to account for these particular transactions.

Selling the stones to Bling Ltd and not making payments in accordance with the prescribed order are two transactions which a liquidator might investigate and seek to set aside, as I have described below.

Sale of stones to Bling Ltd ❸

Although you are not obliged to accept the offer from Bling, it would provide the company with some cash. However, as the £9,000 offered is significantly less than the market price of £40,000, the sale might be considered a transaction at an undervalue. If this sale is made within two years of Jim's Gems being unable to pay its debts, then the liquidator might be able to apply to court to have this transaction 'undone'.

If you, as directors, are able to show that you sold the stones to Bling in good faith, for the purpose of carrying on the business at a time when you genuinely believed the sale would benefit the company, the court may decide *not* to intervene in the sale.

If the directors feel that the £9,000 offered is a reasonable offer, I would suggest that you keep detailed records of the discussions you have had as a board, to show that you did give this careful consideration and were clearly acting in the company's interests and not your own. I note that Fifi does not think it is a valid offer, although she may have conflicting interests in saying this. ❹ You might also consider obtaining other quotes for the items to compare with Bling's offer to verify its reasonableness and provide evidence of the board's considered approach.

Payments to creditors

As I have stated above, if the prescribed priority in which creditors are paid:

   (a) is varied, and someone is paid before they should have been; and
   (b) is made within two years of the company being insolvent or becoming insolvent as a result of the transaction; and
   (c) is made with a desire to deliberately prefer one creditor over another regardless of the statutory priority,

a liquidator can again apply to court to return the property to the company.

Secured creditors (such as Westminster Bank) always rank above unsecured creditors (the stones supplier(s) and the courier company/ies) in the statutory order.

You may be able to argue that the stones suppliers were paid in advance of the Bank to ensure that Jim's Gems had product to sell to enable the company to continue as a going concern, rather than to place the stones supplier(s) in a better position than the Bank. If successfully argued, the stone supplier(s) could be paid first, before Westminster Bank without issue. However, as with the transaction at an undervalue, you should keep clear, detailed records of any discussions you have had as a board in relation to this payment. You should also be mindful of provisions in the Bank's loan agreement that may require you to notify the Bank of any financial troubles, and that failing to do so may result in the loan being repayable immediately. Please send me a copy of the agreement so that I can review it and advise you accordingly.

Personal liability of directors ❺

As directors are the managers of the company, they oversee the day-to-day operations of the business. If they allow the company to continue trading when they know the company to be insolvent, they may be personally liable.

The directors of Jim's Gems all appear to be aware that the company is experiencing financial difficulties and may struggle to pay its debts as they fall due. If you have contracts in the pipeline suggesting that this current financial situation is a short-term measure, then it may be possible to argue that you all do genuinely believe the company will be able to continue trading. However, if this is not the case, and all the directors consider the company's current financial difficulties to continue indefinitely, you should take every step to minimise the potential loss to the company's creditors. Once again, clear records of your board meetings will be important to support your arguments.

Alternative actions available to you ❻

Company directors are under a duty to act in the best interests of the company and to continue the company as a going concern. If, as directors, you genuinely think the business has a prospect of success over time, some options available to you are to:

   - talk to the creditors to see if there is any scope for extending payment terms or getting a brief 'payment holiday'
   - enter into a collective arrangement with all the creditors

- appoint an administrator to take over the running of the company, who might then sell off some assets while aiming to sell the core business as a going concern
- consider a restructuring plan for Jim's Gems.

If, however, you do not feel the company is likely to continue, you should be mindful of your duty not to defraud creditors and take steps to stop trading to avoid personal liability as set out above.

To conclude, I would strongly urge you to liaise with the company's accountants and notify the company's creditors of Jim's Gems' financial issues as soon as possible. You should also ensure that you have clear notes of board meetings and financial discussions with creditors and other third parties. ➐

COMMENTARY

➊ As with the sample answer to question 1, it is important to identify the relevant facts and what the client wants at the beginning of the note.

➋ The section entitled 'Summary of liquidation process' sets out what liquidation is and how it can be initiated. Without this background context, the client would not be able to clearly establish the relevance of trading while insolvent.

➌ The note then goes on to clearly address the client's key concerns: whether or not to accept the offer from Bling, and which order to pay the creditors. It provides client-focused advice. Note how it does not tell the client what to do, but instead sets out the legal position and the options available to the client, applying the law correctly to the client's situation. Note also how the use of headings, 'Sale of stones to Bling' and 'Payments to creditors' assists in providing clear, structured advice to address the client's situation.

➍ The instructions state that Fifi wants the loan of £3,000 to her nephew, Stewart Chan, to be repaid as soon as possible. This may be why Fifi considers the offer of £9,000 from Bling to be unreasonable – the facts do not provide further details. The client is Jim's Gems, not Fifi, so the advice provided must be directed to Jim's Gems. Any possibility that a director is *not* acting in the best interests of the company should be flagged up to our client company. Note also the requirement to apply the law comprehensively to the situation, identifying any professional conduct issues.

➎ The section headed up 'Personal Liability of directors' commences by setting out the relevant law and explaining how this might apply to the directors of the company. This demonstrates a comprehensive understanding of the law and stresses the severity of the issue to the client, providing client-focused advice. It is important to remember that the client is the company and not the individual directors.

➏ The section headed 'Alternative action available to you' provides client-focused, practical, commercial advice, going beyond what the client has specifically asked, but relevant to what the client wants to achieve. Directors of a company facing financial difficulties should consider all the options.

➐ This is concise, comprehensive and client-focused advice, providing a clear steer to the client of what action they should take.

Does this answer meet the threshold?

The sample answer provides client-focused advice, addressing the client's key concerns by setting out the legal position and the options available to the client. The answers to the client's questions are clearly set out, ensuring the advice is comprehensive. It is likely to meet the threshold standard for the SQE2 case and matter analysis assessment.

Now consider the second sample answer to question 2.

■ SAMPLE ANSWER 2 TO QUESTION 2

I am writing about the winding up of Jim's Gems Ltd as I understand you would like a summary of the consequences. **❶** Jim Pope is in a very unfortunate position as managing director of a failing company. **❷**

If a company is experiencing financial difficulties, due to a downturn in the economy, a hike in interest rates, or for any other reason, a liquidator might be appointed. A liquidator has some powers available to them when trying to recover funds to enable the company to continue trading. **❸** In addition, the liquidator may try to set aside certain transactions as those transactions might then be treated as invalid and the assets would revert back to the company, then being available for disposal to pay back the creditors. **❹** The market value of goods is the value they could fetch if sold in the open market without any forced pressure to sell, ideally, a liquidator should seek to obtain the market price for the company's assets it is trying to dispose of. **❺** Accepting £9,000 for the goods when the market value of the items is £40,000 would be considered a transaction at an undervalue if it occurred within a specific time period of the company's insolvency and a liquidator could set aside the transaction. **❻** Similarly, paying unsecured creditors in advance of secured creditors would be a preference and a liquidator could request to the court that it effectively is 'undone'. **❼**

As directors, if you allow the company to trade while insolvent, you could be personally liable under the wrongful or fraudulent trading rules of the Insolvency Act. **❽**

COMMENTARY

❶ The introduction is weak. Jim's Gems is not being wound up yet, although this might happen in the future as a result of its financial difficulties.

❷ As with note 1 above, the company is not yet wound up. It is experiencing financial difficulties, but there are options available to the company before it enters into liquidation. Consequently it is not appropriate to call it a 'failing company'.

❸ This is not legally correct. A liquidator is appointed after a company is insolvent to recover funds from a company in order to pay the company's creditors.

❹ This sentence is legally correct. It sets the context of liquidators' powers.

❺ This is a long sentence that is neither precise nor concise. It is not really answering the client's question and so is not client-focused or providing comprehensive advice.

❻ This does not apply the law correctly or comprehensively to the client's situation. The time period that is relevant to investigating a transaction at an undervalue is not specified. Similarly, no reference is made to when a transaction at an undervalue may be permitted, ie if it is entered into in good faith for the purposes of carrying on the business. The court would determine whether the transaction could be set aside.

❼ Similarly, the final sentence in this paragraph is not entirely correct. There may be instances where the preference is not voidable, such as in the client's situation where payment may have been made to keep the business going.

❽ This final sentence does not explain the law. It does not apply the law comprehensively to the client's situation, nor does it provide client-focused advice. There is no consideration of how the client's directors could avoid actions for wrongful/fraudulent trading. This is also an abrupt ending to the note without suggesting next steps for the client, such as inviting Jim to inform the partner how he would like to proceed.

Does this answer meet the threshold?

It is unlikely that this second answer would meet the threshold standard for the SQE2 case and matter analysis assessment. The advice is not client-focused, important information such as the time period that is relevant to investigating transactions at an undervalue is not addressed, and the law is not applied comprehensively to the client's situation.

■ KEY POINT CHECKLIST

This chapter has covered the following key knowledge points:
- The SQE2 assessment criteria for case and matter analysis and how to apply them in the context of business organisations, rules and procedures.
- The importance of showing you understand the problem from the client's point of view.
- How answers in the format of letters or memoranda could look, which are either likely or unlikely to meet the SQE2 threshold standard, and with full commentary on their strengths and weaknesses.

■ SUMMARY AND REFLECTION

The key to success in the SQE2 case and matter analysis assessment is taking your time to read the question and the facts properly, thinking about the legal issues the question is asking you to address, but also identifying what the client wants to know. You then need to ensure that these points are all addressed with a client-focused approach in your memorandum or report.

Remember that you are being judged on whether you apply the law both correctly and comprehensively *to the client's situation*. It is essential that you consider the relevant law and explain how it is applicable to the client's scenario.

Make sure you practise writing in client-friendly language. Too much legal jargon or legalistic terms used without accompanying explanation will mean that your note is not easily understandable for a client recipient, and you will be penalised for this in the assessment.

Now, take the time to reflect and consider what you might still need to work on, and whether you feel completely confident in your case and matter analysis skills in the context of business organisations, rules and procedures.

2

Legal research

■ MAKE SURE YOU KNOW

This chapter deals with the skill of legal research in the context of business organisations, rules and procedures. It is important to identify what the client wants, and the impact on the client and other stakeholders, as applicable. Shareholders, directors, partners, employees, creditors and debtors are just some examples of parties that may be affected by what is uncovered in your research.

Legal research in this area is one of the skills that will be assessed on day three of the SQE2 assessments (see the Introduction for more detail). The SQE2 can test candidates' knowledge not only of the legal principles and practices associated with business organisations, business taxation, money laundering and financial services, but also the application of contract law to these principles. It is therefore essential that you familiarise yourself with the contents of *Revise SQE: Business Law and Practice* and *Revise SQE Contract Law* before attempting the practice questions in this chapter.

■ SQE ASSESSMENT ADVICE

As you work through this chapter, remember to pay particular attention in your revision to:
• how the relevant facts are included in the sample answers
• ways in which the advice given is tailored to the client/recipient and addresses legal and non-legal approaches
• how the sample answers use precise, concise and acceptable language
• how the law is correctly and comprehensively applied to the client's situation
• the way in which any ethical or professional conduct issues are identified and resolved.

See the Appendix for the SRA's performance indicators in legal research.

■ INTRODUCTION TO LEGAL RESEARCH IN BUSINESS ORGANISATIONS, RULES AND PROCEDURES

The SQE2 assessment will probably replicate scenarios which occur in everyday legal practice. To test your legal research skills, this assessment will be based on reading a memo or email from a partner which asks you to research and provide the correct legal knowledge for them to be able to advise a client. While the question itself will give you some direction about the areas you need to cover in your report, you will be required to apply your knowledge of those areas and your understanding of the resources provided to the scenario, in order to communicate the relevant advice to the instructing partner clearly and concisely in writing. This chapter will provide examples of how you can identify the most appropriate and relevant sources, then extract the pertinent information and apply it to the scenario, so that you can meet the criteria for the SQE2 legal research assessment.

To succeed in your SQE2 legal research assessment, you need to approach the question methodically. Try following these steps:
1. Once you have read all the documentation, write down the question(s) being asked of you.

2. Write down the key facts from the instructions that you feel are relevant to answer the question.
3. Check the dates of the sources and then write down the key law that you think is relevant from the extracts provided, ideally using primary sources (case law and/or statute) over secondary sources (such as extracts from textbooks) wherever possible.
4. Check that the law identified in point 3 above relates back to and answers the question(s) you identified in point 1.
5. Consider how the law was applied to the facts in any case law.
6. Identify key steps applied in the relevant sources and write your answer to the question, ensuring it relates back to and answers the question(s) you identified in point 1 above.
7. Review your answer, keeping in mind the question and the SQE2 legal research assessment criteria.

Assessment technique

When reviewing your answer, read each sentence carefully to make sure it relates back to the question. This technique stops you from applying irrelevant facts and law.

SQE2 legal research assessment criteria

Try to remember these points as you construct your answer:

Skills

1. Identify and use relevant sources and information.
2. Provide advice which is client-focused and addresses the client's problem.
3. Use clear, precise, concise and acceptable language.

Application of law

4. Apply the law correctly to the client's situation.
5. Apply the law comprehensively to the client's situation, identifying any ethical and professional conduct issues and exercising judgement to resolve them honestly and with integrity.

In chapter 2 of **Revise SQE: Business Law and Practice**, we considered the personal liability of directors. Question 1 below demonstrates how your knowledge of this topic could be tested in the context and format of an SQE2 legal research assessment. The sample questions in this chapter include six sources for you to consider, but bear in mind that the SQE2 assessment might include up to eight sources.

■ QUESTION 1

Email to candidate

From: Partner
Sent: 1 March 202#
To: Candidate
Subject: Jeremy Bluer and Xavier Bustamente

I met Jeremy Bluer and Xavier Bustamente today. They are new clients and are both Spanish nationals with indefinite leave to remain and work in the United Kingdom.

Over the last 18 months, they have been employed by Casper Ltd ('Casper') to pick fruit and vegetables and tend to the land of various farms. Jeremy and Xavier believe they were employed by Casper in an exploitative manner, often working very long hours and being paid less than the statutory minimum prescribed. It is common ground that Jeremy's and Xavier's employment by Casper was subject to the regulatory regime under the Gangmasters (Licensing) Act 2004 and the rules made under it.

Abigail Gleeson is the sole director and shareholder of Casper. Fernandez Mowan is Casper's company secretary. There is a great deal of evidence supporting the claim that Abigail alone had been managing Casper at all material times.

Having looked at the evidence Jeremy and Xavier have collected, it is clear that their payslips did not reflect the true hours they worked, sometimes recording just 50-60% of the total actual hours worked. As a result, up to £300 a week was withheld for at least 12 months. The records strongly indicate that Abigail behaved in a deliberate and systematic manner to inaccurately record the hours worked by Jeremy and Xavier, and I believe summary judgment will be granted in their favour.

Jeremy and Xavier would like to know whether they might also be able to bring a claim against Abigail for being personally, jointly and/or severally liable for Casper's breaches of contract.

Could you please research the answer to this question, using the sources provided, and report back to me so that I can prepare my advice for Jeremy and Xavier. I should like you to include for my reference your legal reasoning, mentioning any key sources or authorities.

Many thanks

Partner

Note to candidates:

You do not need to consider the rules and regulations under the Gangmasters (Licensing) Act 2004 nor the validity of Jeremy's and Xavier's status in the UK.

Given the time constraints of this assessment, we have not provided the full text of some primary sources. Where the full text of a primary source is not provided, candidates may nevertheless cite the primary source on the basis it is referred to in one or more of the secondary sources provided and the full text can be checked at a later date.

Information displayed is as obtained on the date of search, for example purposes only. Information contained herein is not to be relied upon outside of the purposes of this sample question.

Attachments
You have been provided with the following sources listed alphabetically in order of source name. The order of presentation is not intended as a guide to the order in which they should be consulted.

PLEASE NOTE THAT PART OR ALL OF SOME OF THESE SOURCES MAY NOT BE RELEVANT TO ANSWERING THE QUESTION.

1. *Antuzis and others v DJ Houghton Catching Services Ltd and others* [2019] EWHC 843 (QB)
2. Companies Act 2006 ss 172-175

3. Company Directors Disqualification Act 1986 ss 6–8
4. Gangmasters (Licensing) Act 2004 ss 4, 6, 7
5. *Gore-Browne on Companies*, Part II Constitution and personality, Chapter 7A Attribution and crimes
6. *Halsbury's Laws of England*, Companies, Vol. 14, para 275.

*   *   *

Source 1

Contains public sector information licensed under the Open Government Licence v3.0. Note that in this judgment, D1 is the company; D2 and D3 are officers of the company.

Antuzis and others v DJ Houghton Catching Services Ltd and others [2019] EWHC 843 (QB)

Queen's Bench Division
Lane J

8 April 2019

A. INTRODUCTION

2. The claimants further contend that they were frequently not paid the sums which were recorded as being due to them on their respective pay slips, which had in any event been calculated on a fictional basis. Payments were often withheld as a form of punishment for alleged transgressions. D1 made no attempt to pay the claimants holiday pay, to which they were entitled, or to pay overtime at the prescribed rates. Nor was a claimant permitted to take absence on account of bereavement.
3. Deductions were also, the claimants say, unlawfully made in respect of so-called employment fees and for rent, in respect of premises at which the claimants were effectively required to reside, with the rent being in excess of the maximum permitted under the legislation.

B. THE ORDER OF 8 AUGUST 2018

4. On 8 August 2018, Master Yoxall ordered there to be a trial of a preliminary issue; namely whether the second and third defendants (hereafter D2 and D3) are personally, jointly and/or severally liable to the claimants for the D1's breaches of contract. The order stated that 'for the avoidance of doubt reference to claims under "breaches of contract" includes any related claims under statute or statutory instrument'. The present proceedings do not involve the fourth defendant.

F. COMPANIES ACT 2006

43. The final statutory scheme which is necessary to mention is that contained in the Companies Act 2006. Section 172 (duty to promote the success of the company), so far as relevant, provides as follows:
    '(1) A director of a company must act in the way he considers, in good faith, would be most likely to promote the success of the company for the benefit

of its members as a whole, and in doing so have regard (amongst other matters) to –
(a) the likely consequences of any decision in the long term,
(b) the interests of the company's employees,

. . .

(d) the impact of the company's operations on the community and the environment,
(e) the desirability of the company maintaining a reputation for high standards of business conduct, and

. . .'

44. Section 174 (Duty to exercise reasonable care, skill and diligence) provides:
'(1) A director of a company must exercise reasonable care, skill and diligence.
(2) This means the care, skill and diligence that would be exercised by a reasonably diligent person with –
(a) the general knowledge, skill and experience that may reasonably be expected of a person carrying out the functions carried out by the director in relation to the company, and
(b) the general knowledge, skill and experience that the director has.'

55. Although the evidence of the three claimants was in accord on many issues, items of detail varied. Far from undermining their credibility, I consider this underscores the fact that each of them was telling the truth.

K. PRELIMINARY ISSUE

108. The general principle is that directors of a company will be liable for the torts of the company, committed at their direction.
109. In *Rainham Chemical Works v Belvedere Fish Guano Company Ltd* [1921] AC 465, Lord Buckmaster held:

'If the company was really trading independently on its own account, the fact that it was directed by Messrs Feldman and Partridge would not render them responsible for its tortious acts unless, indeed, they were acts expressly directed by them. If . . . those in control expressly directed that a wrongful thing can be done, the individuals as well as the company are responsible for the consequences.' (467)

110. A somewhat different position obtains, however, where the unlawful act is procuring a breach of contract. In *Said v Butt* [1920] 3 KB 497, the plaintiff procured a theatre ticket, which was not in his name, knowing that if his true identity had been known, he would have been refused admission, owing to a dispute between him and the theatre company. McCardie J held that non-disclosure of the fact that the ticket was bought for the plaintiff prevented the sale of the ticket from constituting of contract, the identity of the plaintiff being a material element in its formation. For that reason the action failed.
111.   However, McCardie J made these *obiter* observations:

'But the servant who causes a breach of his master's contract with a third person seems to stand in a wholly different position. He is not a stranger. He is the alter ego of his master. His acts are in law, the acts of his employer. In such a case it is the master himself, by his agent, breaking the contract he has made, and in my view the action against the agent . . . must therefore fail just as it would fail if brought against the master himself for wrongly procuring a breach of his own contract . . . .

I hold that if a servant acting bona fide within the scope of his authority procures or causes the breach of a contract between his employer and a third person, he does not become liable to an action of tort at the suit of the person whose contract has thereby been broken. I abstain from expressing any opinion as to the law which may apply if a servant, acting as an entire stranger, wholly outside the range of his powers, procures his master to wrongfully break a contract with a third person.

112.   The so-called rule in *Said v Butt* has been the subject of considerable judicial and academic scrutiny, in the years that followed.

113.   54 . . . Although *Said v Butt* concerned the tort of inducement of breach of contract, which was the applicable tort in that case, its application has been extended to other torts involving a company's breach of contract, such as unlawful means conspiracy where the unlawful means pertains to the contractual breach: see *O'Brien v Dawson* at [58] below.

      55 However, there has thus far been no detailed analysis by the courts of what precisely the principle entails, in particular what it means to act *'bona fide within the scope of [the director's] authority'*. Previous decisions of our courts have interpreted the *Said v Butt* principle to comprise two conjunctive requirements namely: (a) acting *bona fide*; and (b) acting within the scope of the director's authority, and to apply only to 'protect persons in authority within corporate entities who genuinely and honestly endeavoured to act in the company's best interests': see *Chong Hon Kuan* at [49] and *Nagase* at [9]. Thus in *Nagase*, where the company's director, through the company, fraudulently overcharged the plaintiff, the director was held not to be entitled to the protection of the principle.

      56 Conversely, a director who acts in good faith and within his authority would be immune from tortious liability, notwithstanding that he may have been genuinely mistaken as to the company's contractual obligations or even that he had the predominant intention of causing loss to another. An example of the former is the case of *Ng Joo Soon (alias Nga Ju Soon) v Dovechem Holdings Pte Ltd and another suit* [2011] 2 SLR 1155 ('*Ng Joo Soon*'), where the plaintiff sued the company's directors in the tort of inducement of breach of contract and in conspiracy for the wrongful breach of the company's obligation to pay the plaintiff certain sums under a contract. Philip Pillai J held (at [77]) that the directors were immune from such liability as they had acted within their authority and in good faith, and it thus did not matter that they had been mistaken as to the company's contractual obligations.

130.   In short, D2 and D3 were not acting *bona fide* vis-à-vis D1. It is, accordingly, necessary to turn to *OBG Ltd and Another v Allan and others* [2007] UKHL 21 in order of determine whether D2 and/or D3, acting in their own right, are liable for inducing breach of contract.

131.   For our purposes, the following passage of the judgment of Lord Hoffman is relevant:

      '39. To be liable for inducing breach of contract, you must know that you are inducing a breach of contract. It is not enough that you know that you are procuring an act which, as a matter of law or construction of the contract, is a breach. You must actually realize that it will have this effect. Nor does it matter that you ought reasonably to have done so. This proposition is most strikingly illustrated by the decision of this House in *British Industrial Plastics Ltd v Ferguson* [1940] 1 All ER 479, in which the plaintiff's former employee offered the defendant information about one of the plaintiff's secret processes which he, as an employee, had invented. The defendant knew that the employee had a contractual obligation not to reveal trade secrets but held the eccentric opinion that if the process was patentable, it would be the exclusive property of the employee. He took the information in the honest belief that the employee would not be in breach of contract. In the Court of Appeal McKinnon LJ observed tartly ([1938] 4 All ER 504, 513) that in accepting this evidence the judge had 'vindicated [his] honesty . . . at the expense of his intelligence' but he and the House of Lords agreed that he could not be held liable for inducing a breach of contract.'

132. I have no hesitation in finding that both D2 and D3 satisfy the requirements laid out by Lord Hoffmann. I am in no doubt whatsoever, having heard the evidence, that both of them 'actually realised' that what they were doing involved causing D1 to breach its contractual obligations towards the claimants. What they did was the means to an end. There is no iota of credible evidence that either D2 or D3 possessed an honest belief that what they were doing would not involve such a breach. On the contrary, the evidence is overwhelmingly to the contrary. At all material times, each knew exactly what he or she was doing. The breaches they occasioned were central to D1's *modus operandi*.

133. Judgment in the preliminary issue will be entered in favour of the claimants. D2 and D3 are jointly and severally liable to the claimants for inducing the breaches of contract of D1.

* * *

Source 2

Companies Act 2006

172 Duty to promote the success of the company

(1) A director of a company must act in the way he considers, in good faith, would be most likely to promote the success of the company for the benefit of its members as a whole, and in doing so have regard (amongst other matters) to:
(a) the likely consequences of any decision in the long term,
(b) the interests of the company's employees,
(c) the need to foster the company's business relationships with suppliers, customers and others,
(d) the impact of the company's operations on the community and the environment,
(e) the desirability of the company maintaining a reputation for high standards of business conduct, and
(f) the need to act fairly as between members of the company.
(2) Where or to the extent that the purposes of the company consist of or include purposes other than the benefit of its members, subsection (1) has effect as if the reference to promoting the success of the company for the benefit of its members were to achieving those purposes.
(3) The duty imposed by this section has effect subject to any enactment or rule of law requiring directors, in certain circumstances, to consider or act in the interests of creditors of the company.

173   Duty to exercise independent judgment

(1) A director of a company must exercise independent judgment.
(2) This duty is not infringed by his acting:
  (a) in accordance with an agreement duly entered into by the company that restricts the future exercise of discretion by its directors, or
  (b) in a way authorised by the company's constitution.

174   Duty to exercise reasonable care, skill and diligence

(1) A director of a company must exercise reasonable care, skill and diligence.
(2) This means the care, skill and diligence that would be exercised by a reasonably diligent person with
  (a) the general knowledge, skill and experience that may reasonably be expected of a person carrying out the functions carried out by the director in relation to the company, and
  (b) the general knowledge, skill and experience that the director has.

175   Duty to avoid conflicts of interest

(1) A director of a company must avoid a situation in which he has, or can have, a direct or indirect interest that conflicts, or possibly may conflict, with the interests of the company.
(2) This applies in particular to the exploitation of any property, information or opportunity (and it is immaterial whether the company could take advantage of the property, information or opportunity).
(3) This duty does not apply to a conflict of interest arising in relation to a transaction or arrangement with the company.
(4) This duty is not infringed:
  (a) if the situation cannot reasonably be regarded as likely to give rise to a conflict of interest; or
  (b) if the matter has been authorised by the directors.
(5) Authorisation may be given by the directors:
  (a) where the company is a private company and nothing in the company's constitution invalidates such authorisation, by the matter being proposed to and authorised by the directors; or
  (b) where the company is a public company and its constitution includes provision enabling the directors to authorise the matter, by the matter being proposed to and authorised by them in accordance with the constitution.
(6) The authorisation is effective only if:
  (a) any requirement as to the quorum at the meeting at which the matter is considered is met without counting the director in question or any other interested director, and
  (b) the matter was agreed to without their voting or would have been agreed to if their votes had not been counted.
(7) Any reference in this section to a conflict of interest includes a conflict of interest and duty and a conflict of duties.

* * *

Source 3

Contains public sector information licensed under the Open Government Licence v3.0.

Company Directors Disqualification Act 1986

Disqualification for unfitness

6   Duty of court to disqualify unfit directors F1 . . . .

(1) The court shall make a disqualification order against a person in any case where, on an application under this section **F2** . . .

[F3 (a) the court is satisfied:

(i) that the person is or has been a director of a company which has at any time become insolvent (whether while the person was a director or subsequently), or

(ii) that the person has been a director of a company which has at any time been dissolved without becoming insolvent (whether while the person was a director or subsequently), and**]**

[F3 (b) the court is satisfied that the person's conduct as a director of that company (either taken alone or taken together with the person's conduct as a director of one or more other companies or overseas companies) makes the person unfit to be concerned in the management of a company.**]**

[F4 (1A) In this section references to a person's conduct as a director of any company or overseas company include, where that company or overseas company has become insolvent, references to that person's conduct in relation to any matter connected with or arising out of the insolvency.**]**

(2) For the purposes of this section **F5** . . ., a company becomes insolvent if:

(a) the company goes into liquidation at a time when its assets are insufficient for the payment of its debts and other liabilities and the expenses of the winding up,

[F6 (b) the company enters administration,**]**

(c) an administrative receiver of the company is appointed;

F7. . . . .

[F8 (2A) For the purposes of this section, an overseas company becomes insolvent if the company enters into insolvency proceedings of any description (including interim proceedings) in any jurisdiction.**]**

[F9 (3) In this section and section 7(2), 'the court' means:

(a) where the company in question is being or has been wound up by the court, that court,

(b) where the company in question is being or has been wound up voluntarily, any court which has or (as the case may be) had jurisdiction to wind it up**]**,

[F10 (c) where neither paragraph (a) nor (b) applies but an administrator or administrative receiver has at any time been appointed in respect of the company in question, any court which has jurisdiction to wind it up**]**,

[F11 (d) where the company in question has been dissolved without becoming insolvent, a court which at the time it was dissolved had jurisdiction to wind it up.**]**

(3A) Sections 117 and 120 of the **M1** Insolvency Act 1986 (jurisdiction) shall apply for the purposes of subsection (3) as if the references in the definitions of 'registered office' to the presentation of the petition for winding up were references:

(a) in a case within paragraph (b) of that subsection, to the passing of the resolution for voluntary winding up,

[F12 (b) in a case within paragraph (c) of that subsection, to the appointment of the administrator or (as the case may be) administrative receiver.**]**

(3B) Nothing in subsection (3) invalidates any proceedings by reason of their being taken in the wrong court; and proceedings:

(a) for or in connection with a disqualification order under this section, or

(b) in connection with a disqualification undertaking accepted under section 7, may be retained in the court in which the proceedings were commenced, although it may not be the court in which they ought to have been commenced.

(3C) In this section and section 7, 'director' includes a shadow director**]**

(4) Under this section the minimum period of disqualification is two years, and the maximum period is 15 years.

7   **[F13** Disqualification orders under section 6: applications and acceptance of undertakings**]**

(1) If it appears to the Secretary of State that it is expedient in the public interest that a disqualification order under section 6 should be made against any person, an application for the making of such an order against that person may be made:

(a) by the Secretary of State, or

(b) if the Secretary of State so directs in the case of a person who is or has been a director of a company which is being **[F14** or has been**]** wound up by the court in England and Wales, by the official receiver.

(2) Except with the leave of the court, an application for the making under that section of a disqualification order against any person shall not be made after the end of the period of **[F15** 3 years**]** beginning with **[F16**:

(a) in a case where the person is or has been a director of a company which has become insolvent, the day on which the company became insolvent, or

(b) in a case where the person has been a director of a company which has been dissolved without becoming insolvent, the day on which the company was dissolved.**]**

[F17 (2A) If it appears to the Secretary of State that the conditions mentioned in section 6(1) are satisfied as respects any person who has offered to give him a disqualification undertaking, he may accept the undertaking if it appears to him that it is expedient in the public interest that he should do so (instead of applying, or proceeding with an application, for a disqualification order).**]**

F18 (3). . . . .

(4) The Secretary of State or the official receiver may require **[F19** any person**]**:

(a) to furnish him with such information with respect to **[F20** that person's or another person's conduct as a director of a company which has at any time become insolvent **[F21** or been dissolved without becoming insolvent**]** (whether while the person was a director or subsequently), and**]**

(b) to produce and permit inspection of such books, papers and other records **[F22** as are considered by the Secretary of State or (as the case may be) the official receiver to be relevant to that person's or another person's conduct as such a director**]**,

as the Secretary of State or the official receiver may reasonably require for the purpose of determining whether to exercise, or of exercising, any function of his under this section.

[F23 (5) Subsections (1A) and (2) of section 6 apply for the purposes of this section as they apply for the purposes of that section.**]**

[F24 7A Office-holder's report on conduct of directors

(1) The office-holder in respect of a company which is insolvent must prepare a report (a 'conduct report') about the conduct of each person who was a director of the company:

(a) on the insolvency date, or

(b) at any time during the period of three years ending with that date.

(2) For the purposes of this section a company is insolvent if:

(a) the company is in liquidation and at the time it went into liquidation its assets were insufficient for the payment of its debts and other liabilities and the expenses of the winding up,

(b) the company has entered administration, or

(c) an administrative receiver of the company has been appointed;

and subsection (1A) of section 6 applies for the purposes of this section as it applies for the purpose of that section.

(3) A conduct report must, in relation to each person, describe any conduct of the person which may assist the Secretary of State in deciding whether to exercise the power under section 7(1) or (2A) in relation to the person.

(4) The office-holder must send the conduct report to the Secretary of State before the end of:

(a) the period of 3 months beginning with the insolvency date, or

(b) such other longer period as the Secretary of State considers appropriate in the particular circumstances.

(5) If new information comes to the attention of an office-holder, the office-holder must send that information to the Secretary of State as soon as reasonably practicable.

(6) 'New information' is information which an office-holder considers should have been included in a conduct report prepared in relation to the company, or would have been so included had it been available before the report was sent.

(7) If there is more than one office-holder in respect of a company at any particular time (because the company is insolvent by virtue of falling within more than one paragraph of subsection (2) at that time), subsection (1) applies only to the first of the office-holders to be appointed.

(8) In the case of a company which is at different times insolvent by virtue of falling within one or more different paragraphs of subsection (2):

(a) the references in subsection (1) to the insolvency date are to be read as references to the first such date during the period in which the company is insolvent, and

(b) subsection (1) does not apply to an office-holder if at any time during the period in which the company is insolvent a conduct report has already been prepared and sent to the Secretary of State.

(9) The 'office-holder' in respect of a company which is insolvent is:

(a) in the case of a company being wound up by the court in England and Wales, the official receiver;

(b) in the case of a company being wound up otherwise, the liquidator;

(c) in the case of a company in administration, the administrator;

(d) in the case of a company of which there is an administrative receiver, the receiver.

(10) The 'insolvency date'

(a) in the case of a company being wound up by the court, means the date on which the court makes the winding-up order (see section 125 of the Insolvency Act 1986);

(b) in the case of a company being wound up by way of a members' voluntary winding up, means the date on which the liquidator forms the opinion that the company will be unable to pay its debts in full (together with interest at the official rate) within the period stated in the directors' declaration of solvency under section 89 of the Insolvency Act 1986;

(c) in the case of a company being wound up by way of a creditors' voluntary winding up where no such declaration under section 89 of that Act has been made, means the date of the passing of the resolution for voluntary winding up;

(d) in the case of a company which has entered administration, means the date the company did so;

(e) in the case of a company in respect of which an administrative receiver has been appointed, means the date of that appointment.

(11) For the purposes of subsection (10)(e), any appointment of an administrative receiver to replace an administrative receiver who has died or vacated office pursuant to section 45 of the Insolvency Act 1986 is to be ignored.

(12) In this section:
- 'court' has the same meaning as in section 6;
- 'director' includes a shadow director.]

8   [F25 Disqualification of director on finding of unfitness.]

[F26 (1) If it appears to the Secretary of State **F27** . . . that it is expedient in the public interest that a disqualification order should be made against a person who is, or has been, a director or shadow director of a company, he may apply to the court for such an order.

F28 (1A) . . . .]

(2) The court may make a disqualification order against a person where, on an application under this section, it is satisfied that his conduct in relation to the company **[F29** (either taken alone or taken together with his conduct as a director or shadow director of one or more other companies or overseas companies)] makes him unfit to be concerned in the management of a company.

[F30 (2A) Where it appears to the Secretary of State **F31** . . . that, in the case of a person who has offered to give him a disqualification undertaking:

(a) the conduct of the person in relation to a company of which the person is or has been a director or shadow director **[F32** (either taken alone or taken together with his conduct as a director or shadow director of one or more other companies or overseas companies)] makes him unfit to be concerned in the management of a company, and

(b) it is expedient in the public interest that he should accept the undertaking (instead of applying, or proceeding with an application, for a disqualification order), he may accept the undertaking.]

[F33 (2B) Subsection (1A) of section 6 applies for the purposes of this section as it applies for the purposes of that section.]

(3) In this section 'the court' means the High Court or, in Scotland, the Court of Session.

(4) The maximum period of disqualification under this section is 15 years.

* * *

Source 4

Gangmasters (Licensing) Act 2004

4   Acting as a gangmaster

(1) This section defines what is meant in this Act by a person acting as a gangmaster.

(2) A person ('A') acts as a gangmaster if he supplies a worker to do work to which this Act applies for another person ('B').

(3) For the purposes of subsection (2) it does not matter:

(a) whether the worker works under a contract with A or is supplied to him by another person,

(b) whether the worker is supplied directly under arrangements between A and B or indirectly under arrangements involving one or more intermediaries,

(c) whether A supplies the worker himself or procures that the worker is supplied,

(d) whether the work is done under the control of A, B or an intermediary,

(e) whether the work done for B is for the purposes of a business carried on by him or in connection with services provided by him to another person.

(4) A person ('A') acts as a gangmaster if he uses a worker to do work to which this Act applies in connection with services provided by him to another person.

(5) A person ('A') acts as a gangmaster if he uses a worker to do any of the following work to which this Act applies for the purposes of a business carried on by him:

(a) harvesting or otherwise gathering agricultural produce following –

(i) a sale, assignment or lease of produce to A, or

(ii) the making of any other agreement with A,

where the sale, assignment, lease or other agreement was entered into for the purpose of enabling the harvesting or gathering to take place;

(b) gathering shellfish;

(c) processing or packaging agricultural produce harvested or gathered as mentioned in paragraph (a).

In this subsection 'agricultural produce' means any produce derived from agriculture.

(6) For the purposes of subsection (4) or (5) A shall be treated as using a worker to do work to which this Act applies if he makes arrangements under which the worker does the work –

(a) whether the worker works for A (or for another) or on his own account, and

(b) whether or not he works under a contract (with A or another).

(7) Regulations under section 3(5)(b) may provide for the application of subsections (5) and (6) above in relation to work that is work to which this Act applies by virtue of the regulations.

LICENSING

6 Prohibition of unlicensed activities

(1) A person shall not act as a gangmaster except under the authority of a licence.

(2) Regulations made by the Secretary of State may specify circumstances in which a licence is not required.

Chapter 11

An Act to make provision for the licensing of activities involving the supply or use of workers in connection with agricultural work, the gathering of wild creatures and wild plants, the harvesting of fish from fish farms, and certain processing and packaging; and for connected purposes.

7 Grant of licence

(1) The Authority may grant a licence if it thinks fit.

(2) A licence shall describe the activities authorised by it and shall be granted for such period as the Authority thinks fit.

(3) A licence authorises activities –

(a) by the holder of the licence, and

(b) by persons employed or engaged by the holder of the licence who are named or otherwise specified in the licence.

(4) In the case of a licence held otherwise than by an individual, the reference in subsection (3)(a) to activities by the holder of the licence shall be read as a reference only to such activities as are mentioned in whichever of the following provisions applies:

section 20(2) (body corporate);
section 21(2) (unincorporated association);
section 22(4) (partnership that is regarded as a legal person under the law of the country or territory under which it is formed).

(5) A licence shall be granted subject to such conditions as the Authority considers appropriate.

* * *

Source 5

Gore-Browne on Companies, Part II Constitution and personality, Chapter 7A Attribution and crimes

Williams v Natural Life

[13]

In *Williams v Natural Life Health Foods*,[1] the House of Lords, overruling the Court of Appeal,[2] carefully restricted the circumstances in which a director of a company would be personally liable to plaintiffs for loss which they suffered as a result of negligent advice given to them by the company. First, there had to be an assumption of responsibility. This assumption had to be determined objectively. The primary focus had to be on exchanges (including statements and conduct) between the director and the plaintiffs. Secondly, the test of reliance on the assumption was not simply one of reliance in fact but whether the plaintiffs could reasonably rely on the assumption of responsibility.

The action in *Williams* was originally brought primarily against the company on the basis of the 'extended *Hedley Byrne* principle' established by the House of Lords in *Henderson v Merrett Syndicates Ltd*.[3] This decision settled that the assumption of responsibility principle enunciated in *Hedley Byrne* is not confined to statements but may apply to any assumption of responsibility for the provision of services.[4] In *Williams* the company, after judgment for financial loss had been obtained against it, became insolvent and was wound up. The proceedings were continued instead against the defendant director when the judgment against the company remained unsatisfied.

The House of Lords concluded that in the circumstances of *Williams*, the director had not assumed personal responsibility.[5] Although in the Court of Appeal, Waite LJ emphasised the need to restrict tortious liability in these circumstances 'lest the protection of incorporation should be virtually nullified',[6] Lord Steyn, giving the only judgment in the House of Lords, said:

the issue in this case is not peculiar to companies. Whether the principal is a company or a natural person, someone acting on his behalf may incur personal liability in tort as well as imposing vicarious or attributed liability upon his principal. But in order to establish personal liability under the principle of *Hedley Byrne*, which requires the existence of a special relationship between plaintiff and tortfeasor, it is not sufficient that there should have been a special relationship with the principal. There must have been an assumption of responsibility such as to create a special relationship with the director or employee himself.[7]

Williams highlights the tension between the two general rules of attribution and treats liability for negligence on the part of any agent, which causes economic loss, more as a breach of a quasi-contractual (ie voluntarily assumed) than a tortious duty.

---

[1] *[1998] 2 All ER 577, [1998] 1 WLR 830*, HL. See further the cases discussed at 15[1].
[2] *[1997] 1 BCLC 131*. See the judgment of Hirst LJ at 152, where a more flexible approach to imposing tort liability on a director was taken.
[3] *[1995] 2 AC 145*.
[4] See Lord Steyn, *[1998] 1 BCLC 689 at 693-694*. The other members of the court concurred in Lord Steyn's judgment.
[5] *[1998] 2 All ER 577 at 585*.
[6] *[1997] 1 BCLC 131 at 152*.
[7] *[1998] 2 All ER 577 at 582*. This stress on assuming personal responsibility is found in the House of Lords decision in *Henderson v Merrett Syndicates Ltd* [1995] AC 145, but not in other House of Lords decisions such as *Smith v Eric S Bush* [1990] 1 AC 831, *White v Jones* [1995] 2 AC 207, nor even in quite these terms in *Caparo Industries plc v Dickman* [1990] 2 AC 605.

Subsequent cases

[14]

In *Standard Chartered Bank v Pakistan National Shipping Corp*,[1] it was made clear that the normal vicarious liability rules apply where a director was not merely negligent but deceitful so that the director and his company were both liable for any economic loss. So, where a director negotiating an agreement on behalf of the company is deceitful to the future creditor about the company's ability to pay, the director may be personally liable to that creditor, and the Statute of Frauds (Amendment) Act 1828, s 6 is no defence.[2]

In *Partco Group Ltd v Wragg*,[3] it was held that joint liability could arise for negligence causing economic loss where personal responsibility had on the facts been assumed by a director or other agent.[4] In *Merrett v Babb*,[5] a surveyor was held personally liable for his firm's negligent survey but he had signed the survey in his personal capacity. However, there does seem to be an important restriction on such cases of joint liability.

In *MCA Records Inc v Charly Records Ltd (No 5)*, Chadwick LJ said:[6]

> A director will not be treated as liable with the company as a joint tortfeasor if he does no more than carry out his constitutional role in the governance of the company – that is to say, by voting at board meetings. That, I think is what policy requires if a proper recognition is to be given to the identity of the company as a separate legal person. Nor, as it seems to me, will it be right to hold a controlling shareholder liable as a joint tortfeasor if he does no more than exercise his power of control through the constitutional organs of the company – for example by voting at general meetings and by exercising the powers to appoint directors.

The Court of Appeal relied heavily on its previous judgment in the *Standard Chartered* case, which was later reversed in the House of Lords, but this approach has subsequently been reaffirmed in a patent case, *Koninklijke Philips Electronics NV v Princo Digital Disc GmbH*.[7] However, on the facts in both *MCA Records* and *Philips*, the directors concerned were held to have been sufficiently involved beyond the decisions they took as part of the board to be jointly liable.

---

[1] *[2002] UKHL 43, [2003] 1 BCLC 244.*
[2] *Contex Drouzbha Ltd v Wiseman [2007] EWCA Civ 1201, [2008] 1 BCLC 631.*
[3] *Partco Group Ltd v Wragg [2002] 2 BCLC 323, CA*, although the striking-out action only failed because there had been private negotiations between the complainants and the directors, see 43[27].
[4] It has been said in *S Maclise Enterprises Inc v Union Securities Ltd [2008] ABQB 214* (CANLII) by the Alberta Court of Queen's Bench that if a director who is also a shareholder with a very large personal stake in any outcome of the investment in the company is negligent in describing the company to potential investors, the director will be personally liable.
[5] *[2001] QB 1174.*
[6] *[2001] EWCA Civ 1441, [2003] 1 BCLC 93 at 116.* See also *Mentmore Manufacturing Co Ltd v National Merchandising Manufacturing Co Inc (1978) 89 DLR (3d) 195.*
[7] *[2003] EWHC 2588 (Ch), [2004] 2 BCLC 50.*

* * *

Source 6

Halsbury's Laws of England, Companies (Volume 14 (2023), paras 1–467; Volume 14A (2023), paras 468–919; Volume 15 (2023), paras 920–1445; Volume 15A (2023), paras 1446–1924), 2. Companies registered under the Companies Acts, (9) Capacity of company, (iii) Company acting through agents

275. Agent's liability for torts

An agent who commits a tort in the course of his employment is himself liable in damages to the full amount,[1] and, if more than one agent, each agent is so liable.[2] This applies to a company's agent in the same way as to any person's agent; but one of two or more agents is not liable for the acts of the other or others unless he has expressly or impliedly authorised such acts.[3]

Directors are not responsible to third persons for torts committed by sub-agents of the company properly appointed, unless they themselves committed or knowingly procured the commission of the tortious acts.[4]

---

[1] As to the liability of an agent for torts generally see AGENCY VOL 1 (2022) PARA 165.
[2] An officer of the company may be a joint tortfeasor with the company itself: *The Radiant* [1958] 2 Lloyd's Rep 596 (managing director aware of defects in equipment which contributed to accident); *C Evans & Sons Ltd v Spritebrand Ltd* [1985] 2 All ER 415, [1985] 1 WLR 317, CA. As to proceedings against and contributions between joint and several tortfeasors see the Civil

Liability (Contribution) Act 1978; and TORT VOL 97A (2021) PARA 49 et seq.
³ See *Cargill v Bower* (1878) 10 ChD 502; and AGENCY VOL 1 (2022) PARA 28.
⁴ *Weir v Bell* (1878) 3 ExD 238, CA; *Betts v De Vitre* (1868) 3 Ch App 429 at 441, CA, per Lord Chelmsford LC; *Cargill v Bower* (1878) 10 ChD 502; *The Radiant* [1958] 2 Lloyd's Rep 596.
As to the liability of directors for the torts of a company see PARA 632.
As to directors' personal liability for breach of a duty in tort see PARA 635.
As to the ratification of an agent's act by a principal generally see AGENCY VOL 1 (2022) PARAS 58-60, 151 et seq.

* * *

■ YOUR TURN

Have a go at answering question 1, remembering the guidance on pages 19-20.
• Create a list of the relevant legal points raised by the question.
• Create a list of the relevant answers to the legal points provided in the sources and information, remembering to use primary sources over secondary wherever possible.
• Timings are important: you will need to prepare and write your answer in one hour.

SQE1 Functioning legal knowledge link

Remember from chapter 4 of **Revise SQE: Business Law and Practice** that directors owe fiduciary duties to their company. They also have general statutory duties under ss 170-180 Companies Act (CA) 2006. Section 172 CA 2006 requires directors to act in a way *they consider* in good faith would be most likely to promote the success of the company, for the benefit of the members as a whole.

EVALUATING YOUR ANSWER

When you have attempted question 1, mark it yourself against the SQE2 legal research assessment criteria. Do you think your attempt met the threshold standard?

Now compare your attempt with the following key legal points and the sample answers to question 1. A circled number indicates that commentary is provided for this part of the answer. The commentary will explain whether or not the sample is likely to meet the threshold SQE2 standard.

➡Key legal points: Question 1

Note, references to CA 2006 are references to the Companies Act 2006.

In this assessment, part, or all, of the following sources are relevant to the question:

• *Antuzis and others v DJ Houghton Catching Services Ltd and others* [2019] EWHC 843 (QB)
• Companies Act 2006 ss 172 and 174
• *Halsbury's Laws of England*, Companies, Vol. 14, para 275.

The following sources are not relevant to the question:

• Companies Act 2006 ss 173 and 175
• Company Directors Disqualification Act 1986 ss 6-8

- Gangmasters (Licensing) Act 2004 ss 4, 6, 7
- *Gore-Browne on Companies*, Part II Constitution and personality, Chapter 7A Attribution and crimes.

While the reference to *Halsbury's Laws* is relevant to answering the question, the liability of directors who knowingly encourage the company to breach a contract is addressed more specifically in the case of *Antuzis*. Where the primary sources are provided in addition to a commentary on those sources, you should rely on the primary sources.

Key legal points include the following:

- Company directors owe fiduciary duties to their company as set out in ss 170–180 CA 2006. These include the duty to promote the success of the company by acting in good faith (s 172 CA 2006) and the duty to exercise reasonable care, skill and diligence (s 174 CA 2006).
- The general principle is that directors of a company will be liable for the torts of the company committed at their direction (*Rainham Chemical Works v Belvedere Fish Guano Company Ltd* [1921] AC 465).
- The *Said v Butt* principle exempts directors from personal liability for the contractual breaches of their company (whether through the tort of inducement of breach of contract or unlawful means conspiracy) if their acts, in their capacity as directors, are not in themselves in breach of any fiduciary or other personal legal duties owed to the company.
- The nature of the breach and its consequences may directly inform whether the officer of the company has breached their duties towards the company and complied with s 172 CA 2006.
- If the officers of a company do not act bona fide vis-à-vis the company, it is necessary to consider their actions in their own right, to determine their liability (*Antuzis*).
- To be liable for inducing breach of contract, the defendant must know they are causing a breach of the contract or have the means of acquiring such knowledge, which they deliberately disregard (*Antuzis*).

■ SAMPLE ANSWER 1 TO QUESTION 1

Jeremy and Xavier have been employed by Casper Ltd ('Casper') over the last 18 months. Their payslips frequently under-reported the hours they actually worked. I understand that there is overwhelming evidence that Casper's sole director and only shareholder, Abigail Gleeson, supported this deliberate under-recording and that summary judgment is likely to be granted in favour of our clients. ❶

I have researched whether Jeremy and Xavier might be able to bring a claim against Abigail personally for Casper's breaches of contract. ❷

As a director of Casper, Abigail has to comply with some statutory duties. In particular, in accordance with s 172 Companies Act 2006 (CA 2006), she has a duty to promote the success of the company for the benefit of its members as a whole, by acting in good faith. Directors should have regard to (amongst other matters) the interests of the company's employees and the desirability of the company maintaining a reputation for high standards of business conduct (s 172(1)(b) CA 2006). In addition, a director has a duty to exercise reasonable care, skill and diligence under s 174 CA 2006. ❸

Abigail's deliberate under-recording of time might benefit her as the only shareholder, but the practice is clearly not in the interests of the company's employees, who would be receiving an underpayment, nor does it maintain or enhance Casper's business reputation as it suggests that Casper treats its employees unfairly. Abigail's encouragement of the improper reporting could be considered a failure on her part to exercise reasonable skill and diligence. Abigail is therefore likely to be in breach of her duties as a company director as set out in ss 172 and 174 CA 2006. ❹

While directors acting in good faith might be exempt from personal liability for contractual breaches of the company, this would not apply to Abigail. ❺ Abigail knew Casper was incorrectly recording Jeremy's and Xavier's working hours and underpaying them, and she was actively encouraging the continuation of this practice. ❻

In *Rainham Chemical Works v Belvedere Fish Guano Company Ltd* [1921] AC 465, Lord Buckmaster held: 'If ... those in control expressly directed that a wrongful thing can be done, the individuals as well as the company are responsible for the consequences' (467). Here, Abigail was in control and she did expressly direct that the hours be recorded (or not recorded) in a particular way, making her and the company responsible for the consequences. ❼

In *Antuzis and others v DJ Houghton Catching Services Ltd and others* [2019] EWHC 843 (QB), it was held that the officers of the company knew exactly what they were doing at all material times when procuring the company breach its contract. Accordingly the officers were jointly and severally liable for the company breaching its contract. As Casper's sole director, Abigail knew exactly what the company was doing in under-reporting the hours worked by Jeremy and Xavier, and so Abigail is likely to be jointly and severally liable for Casper's breaching its contract with its employees. ❽

COMMENTARY

❶ The opening paragraph sets out the key facts, introducing the clients, company and sole director by name. This provides some context to the advice that follows.

❷ This paragraph summarises the issue on which advice is sought, demonstrating an understanding of the clients' problem from the clients' perspective.

❸ The relevant statute from the sources is identified and the appropriate statutory references are set out, to support the answer to the question. Primary rather than secondary sources should be relied upon wherever possible.

❹ This is an example of how the law is correctly applied to the clients' situation. Information from the scenario is taken and the law is applied to it, with an explanation of the consequences – namely that the actions of Abigail were not in good faith, nor in the interests of the employees or the company's reputation, which are factors to be considered in applying ss 172 and 174 CA 2006.

❺ The *Said v Butt* principle was referred to in paragraphs 110 to 113 of the judgment of *Antuzis and others v DJ Houghton Catching Services Ltd and others* [2019] EWHC 843 (QB) and should have been identified as being relevant law. The principle, with the condition that the director must have acted in good faith, is explained, demonstrating the relevant law has been extracted.

❻ The principle is then applied to the clients' situation, with an analysis of why the rule would not apply (because Abigail, the director of the company, did not act in good faith).

❼ Case law helps with the interpretation of statute. This particular case was quoted in the judgment of *Antuzis* and is relevant to the clients' situation, so the relevant law is identified and extracted. An explanation of why it is relevant is also provided, demonstrating how it can be applied to the facts.

❽ This paragraph refers to the judgment of *Antuzis*. It states the need for knowledge to procure a breach of contract to establish liability and then applies it to the clients' situation. Abigail was a director who proactively encouraged the incorrect time recordings of the company's employees, and therefore was well aware of this practice. She was acting in bad faith when procuring that the company breach the contract with its employees. The paragraph then concludes by providing a client-focused answer to the clients' question – namely that Abigail would be jointly and severally liable.

Does this answer meet the threshold?

The sample answer above contains all the information that the client requires, and that the candidate has been asked to provide. It provides a clear analysis of the law and how it applies to the client's situation, providing references to correctly identified sources and not including irrelevant references. Throughout the answer, the language adopted is clear, precise, concise and acceptable. It is likely to meet the threshold standard for SQE2 legal research.

Note how each of the assessment criteria for legal research are dealt with and, where appropriate, where the examiner is directed specifically to the areas of the report which deal with those criteria. Remember that this is an assessment and you should show your examiners that you are familiar with the criteria by which you are being assessed.

Now consider the second sample answer to question 1.

■ SAMPLE ANSWER 2 TO QUESTION 1

Casper Ltd sources fruitpickers to work at various farms. Abigail is the only shareholder and the only director of Casper. Casper employed Jeremy Bluer and Xavier Bustamente to work on farms and they did so for 18 months. ❶ Abigail, through Casper, exploited Jeremy and Xavier by making them work long hours, paying them less than the minimum wage and even subjecting them to the regime under the Gangmasters (Licensing) Act. ❷

I have researched whether Jeremy and Xavier might also have a claim against Abigail for being personally, jointly and/or severally liable for Casper's breaches of contract. ❸

Jeremy and Xavier clearly have a claim against Casper for the money they were not paid in respect of hours worked. Abigail would argue that by paying Jeremy and Xavier less, she was enabling the company to generate higher profits and thus comply with s 172(1) Companies Act 2006 (CA 2006) which states: 'A director of a company must act in the way he considers, in good faith, would be most likely to promote the success of the company for the benefit of its members as a whole.' Abigail was a director of the company. She was promoting the success of the company for the benefit of herself as she was the only shareholder and thus the beneficiary of any dividend paid. ❹

In the *Antuzis* judgment at paragraph 55 Lane J states: 'Previous decisions of our courts have interpreted the *Said v Butt* principle to comprise two conjunctive requirements namely: (a) acting bona fide; and (b) acting within the scope of the director's authority, and to apply only to "protect persons in authority within corporate entities who genuinely and honestly endeavoured to act in the company's best interests".' Abigail meets both these requirements – she was acting in the company's best interests to generate maximum profits, and had authority as she was the sole director, so can benefit from the *Said v Butt* principle. ❺

According to *Antuzis*, a director who acts in good faith and within his authority would be immune from tortious liability. Abigail would therefore be immune from tortious liability. She would not be liable for procuring the company to breach its contract with Jeremy and Xavier. This would enable Abigail to be excused from any personal liability for Casper's contractual breaches and so she would not be personally liable. ⑥

If not successful with this argument, Abigail might be found to be personally liable for Casper Ltd's contractual breaches and under the Company Directors Disqualification Act s 6(1)(b) the court could consider Abigail to be unfit to be a director of Casper and disqualify her. ⑦ This would mean that she could be banned from being a company director for a period of time and might also be subject to a fine. ⑧

COMMENTARY

① The company should be referred to consistently as either Casper or Casper Ltd.

② While there is strong evidence to suggest this is true, it cannot absolutely be stated that Casper exploited Jeremy and Xavier and subjected them to the Gangmasters (Licensing) Act regime. It should be made clear that this inference is made from the evidence provided. Further, it is the company, not Abigail, that employed and exploited Jeremy and Xavier.

③ This is just restating the question from the instructions, without any interpretation as to how it might apply to the actual facts.

④ Contributing to a company's profitability is not the only requirement of directors. No reference is made to the factors director must have regard to such as the interests of the company's employees and the company's reputation as set out in s 172(1)(a)–(f) CA 2006. There is no reference to directors' duty set out in s 174 CA 2006 which all directors (including Abigail) are subject. This demonstrates a failure to identify and extract the relevant law from the sources and a failure to apply the law correctly and comprehensively to the clients' situation.

⑤ The key requirement of acting in good faith is omitted in the consideration of the principle of *Said v Butt*. The law has been incorrectly extracted and applied to the clients' situation here as no consideration is given as to whether Abigail acted in good faith. The conclusions reached are incorrect and demonstrate a failure to apply the law correctly to the clients' situation.

⑥ Again, the conclusion reached is incorrect. The reference to 'immune from tortious liability' should be elaborated upon, applying it to the clients' situation to make it more client-friendly and less legalistic. This paragraph answers the clients' question and provides client-focused advice, although the advice is incorrect due to a failure to apply the law correctly to the clients' situation.

⑦ The Company Directors Disqualification Act was *not* relevant. The clients did not ask for the consequences and possible penalties that could be imposed on Abigail. It is important to ensure that the answer focuses on addressing the clients' question. Also, as the start of the advice to the client definitively stated that Abigail and Casper were acting unlawfully, an alternative option if this is incorrect should not be provided. This demonstrates a failure to provide client-focused advice using clear, precise and acceptable language. If there is a possibility that the outcome may be one of two options, that should be made clear at the very beginning of the report and not introduced as an afterthought in case the original advice was incorrect.

⑧ This does not answer the clients' question. See comments for point 7 above.

Does this answer meet the threshold?
When assessing the second report against the SQE2 legal research assessment criteria, it is unlikely that this would meet the threshold standard for the SQE2 legal research assessment. It refers to irrelevant law in places, does not address all the relevant facts and at times applies the law incorrectly to the client's situation. Throughout the answer, the language adopted is clear, although it is not always precise or concise.

As you know, SQE2 can assess any of the areas on the SQE1 Business Law and Practice specification. Below is another example of how a different part of the specification could arise in legal research in the context of business organisations, rules and procedures on SQE2.

■ QUESTION 2

Email to candidate

From: Partner
Sent: 1 April 202#
To: Candidate
Subject: Sangita Shah

Sangita Shah is a regular client of ours. We advised her a few years ago on the incorporation of Chabler Ltd., an investment company providing the full range of brokering services to investors, including the creation of 'long and short contracts for difference'. Sangita is the managing director and also the majority shareholder, holding 45% of the shares in Chabler, and the other two shareholders are Punit Sharma and Jinka Wu who hold 30% and 25% of the shares respectively. The other directors are Felicity Crawford and Roland Rames.

Last month, Sangita identified shares in Matters Ltd as being undervalued – at less than £10 per share. She wrote 'contracts for differences' ('CFDs') for shares in Matters on behalf of Chabler's clients, including Sangita's father. Under the CFD, Chabler agrees to pay a sum equal to any increase in value in share price at the date the contract is 'closed out', while Chabler's clients agree to pay a sum equal to any fall in value in the shares on the 'closed out' date. No fixed 'closing out' date was specified in Chabler's contracts, but Sangita advised her clients it should be within the next six months.

At the closing out date, Chabler's clients (including Sangita's father) can decide whether or not to acquire the relevant shares in Matters, and the shares will be transferred from Matters to the appropriate client as required. Chabler manages its own risk by taking out a contract with Hedge Ltd, referencing the same number and volume of shares as it writes out for its own clients. It never advises Hedge of the names of Chabler's clients with CFDs.

Sangita considered the CFDs to be a sound investment option for her clients, including her family and proceeded with the CFDs on that basis. However, she is now concerned that the CFDs with her family members might raise procedural issues relating to corporate governance.

Sangita would like to know whether her family members buying the shares at the closed out date would constitute a substantial property transaction and need approval of Chabler's shareholders.

Could you please research the answer to this question, using the sources provided, and report back to me so that I can prepare my advice for Sangita. I should like you to include for my reference your legal reasoning, mentioning any key sources or authorities.

Many thanks

Partner

Note to candidates:

You do not need to consider the consequences for Sangita if members' approval of the CFDs is not obtained.

Given the time constraints of this assessment, we have not provided the full text of some primary sources. For the purposes of this assessment, where the full text of a primary source is not provided, candidates may nevertheless cite the primary source on the basis it is referred to in one or more of the secondary sources provided and the full text can be checked at a later date.

Information displayed is as obtained on the date of search, for example purposes only. Information contained herein is not to be relied upon outside of the purposes of this sample question.

Attachments

You have been provided with the following sources listed alphabetically in order of source name. The order of presentation is not intended as a guide to the order in which they should be consulted.

PLEASE NOTE THAT PART OR ALL OF SOME OF THESE SOURCES MAY NOT BE RELEVANT TO ANSWERING THE QUESTION.

1. Companies Act 2006 ss 190, 191, 195, 252, 253, 1163
2. *Encyclopaedia of Forms and Precedents*, Companies, Vol. 11(1)c, 3 Directors' interests
3. *Gore-Browne on Companies*, Part IV Directors and management, Chapter 16 Directors' specific obligations
4. *Halsbury's Laws of England*, Companies, Vol. 14a, para 608
5. *Smithton Ltd (formerly Hobart Capital Markets Ltd) v Naggar* [2014] EWCA Civ 939
6. *Tolley's Company Law Handbook*, Chapter 18 Directors.

*   *   *

Source 1

Contains public sector information licensed under the Open Government Licence v3.0.

Companies Act 2006

Substantial property transactions

190 Substantial property transactions: requirement of members' approval

(1) A company may not enter into an arrangement under which:
  (a) a director of the company or of its holding company, or a person connected with such a director, acquires or is to acquire from the company (directly or indirectly) a substantial non-cash asset, or
  (b) the company acquires or is to acquire a substantial non-cash asset (directly or indirectly) from such a director or a person so connected,
  unless the arrangement has been approved by a resolution of the members of the company or is conditional on such approval being obtained.
  For the meaning of 'substantial non-cash asset' see section 191.

(2) If the director or connected person is a director of the company's holding company or a person connected with such a director, the arrangement must also have been approved by a resolution of the members of the holding company or be conditional on such approval being obtained.

(3) A company shall not be subject to any liability by reason of a failure to obtain approval required by this section.

(4) No approval is required under this section on the part of the members of a body corporate that –

    (a) is not a UK-registered company, or

    (b) is a wholly-owned subsidiary of another body corporate.

(5) For the purposes of this section –

    (a) an arrangement involving more than one non-cash asset, or

    (b) an arrangement that is one of a series involving non-cash assets,

shall be treated as if they involved a non-cash asset of a value equal to the aggregate value of all the non-cash assets involved in the arrangement or, as the case may be, the series.

(6) This section does not apply to a transaction so far as it relates –

    (a) to anything to which a director of a company is entitled under his service contract, or

    (b) to payment for loss of office as defined in section 215 [F1 (payments to which the requirements of Chapter 4 or 4A apply)].

191   Meaning of 'substantial'

(1) This section explains what is meant in section 190 (requirement of approval for substantial property transactions) by a 'substantial' non-cash asset.

(2) An asset is a substantial asset in relation to a company if its value –

    (a) exceeds 10% of the company's asset value and is more than £5,000, or

    (b) exceeds £100,000.

(3) For this purpose a company's 'asset value' at any time is:

    (a) the value of the company's net assets determined by reference to its most recent statutory accounts, or

    (b) if no statutory accounts have been prepared, the amount of the company's called-up share capital.

(4) A company's 'statutory accounts' means its annual accounts prepared in accordance with Part 15, and its 'most recent' statutory accounts means those in relation to which the time for sending them out to members (see section 424) is most recent.

(5) Whether an asset is a substantial asset shall be determined as at the time the arrangement is entered into.

195   Property transactions: civil consequences of contravention

(1) This section applies where a company enters into an arrangement in contravention of section 190 (requirement of members' approval for substantial property transactions).

(2) The arrangement, and any transaction entered into in pursuance of the arrangement (whether by the company or any other person), is voidable at the instance of the company, unless –

    (a) restitution of any money or other asset that was the subject matter of the arrangement or transaction is no longer possible,

    (b) the company has been indemnified in pursuance of this section by any other persons for the loss or damage suffered by it, or

    (c) rights acquired in good faith, for value and without actual notice of the contravention by a person who is not a party to the arrangement or transaction would be affected by the avoidance.

(3) Whether or not the arrangement or any such transaction has been avoided, each of the persons specified in subsection (4) is liable –

    (a) to account to the company for any gain that he has made directly or indirectly by the arrangement or transaction, and

    (b) (jointly and severally with any other person so liable under this section) to indemnify the company for any loss or damage resulting from the arrangement or transaction.

(4) The persons so liable are –

    (a) any director of the company or of its holding company with whom the company entered into the arrangement in contravention of section 190,

    (b) any person with whom the company entered into the arrangement in contravention of that section who is connected with a director of the company or of its holding company,

    (c) the director of the company or of its holding company with whom any such person is connected, and

    (d) any other director of the company who authorised the arrangement or any transaction entered into in pursuance of such an arrangement.

(5) Subsections (3) and (4) are subject to the following two subsections.

(6) In the case of an arrangement entered into by a company in contravention of section 190 with a person connected with a director of the company or of its holding company, that director is not liable by virtue of subsection (4)(c) if he shows that he took all reasonable steps to secure the company's compliance with that section.

(7) In any case –

    (a) a person so connected is not liable by virtue of subsection (4)(b), and

    (b) a director is not liable by virtue of subsection (4)(d),

    if he shows that, at the time the arrangement was entered into, he did not know the relevant circumstances constituting the contravention.

(8) Nothing in this section shall be read as excluding the operation of any other enactment or rule of law by virtue of which the arrangement or transaction may be called in question or any liability to the company may arise.

252 Persons connected with a director

(1) This section defines what is meant by references in this Part to a person being 'connected' with a director of a company (or a director being 'connected' with a person).

(2) The following persons (and only those persons) are connected with a director of a company –

    (a) members of the director's family (see section 253);

    (b) a body corporate with which the director is connected (as defined in section 254);

    (c) a person acting in his capacity as trustee of a trust –

        (i) the beneficiaries of which include the director or a person who by virtue of paragraph (a) or (b) is connected with him, or

        (ii) the terms of which confer a power on the trustees that may be exercised for the benefit of the director or any such person,

    other than a trust for the purposes of an employees' share scheme or a pension scheme;

    (d) a person acting in his capacity as partner –

        (i) of the director, or

        (ii) of a person who, by virtue of paragraph (a), (b) or (c), is connected with that director;

    (e) a firm that is a legal person under the law by which it is governed and in which –

        (i) the director is a partner,

(ii) a partner is a person who, by virtue of paragraph (a), (b) or (c) is connected with the director, or

(iii) a partner is a firm in which the director is a partner or in which there is a partner who, by virtue of paragraph (a), (b) or (c), is connected with the director.

(3) References in this Part to a person connected with a director of a company do not include a person who is himself a director of the company.

253 Members of a director's family

(1) This section defines what is meant by references in this Part to members of a director's family.

(2) For the purposes of this Part the members of a director's family are –

(a) the director's spouse or civil partner;

(b) any other person (whether of a different sex or the same sex) with whom the director lives as partner in an enduring family relationship;

(c) the director's children or step-children;

(d) any children or step-children of a person within paragraph (b) (and who are not children or step-children of the director) who live with the director and have not attained the age of 18;

(e) the director's parents.

(3) Subsection (2)(b) does not apply if the other person is the director's grandparent or grandchild, sister, brother, aunt or uncle, or nephew or niece.

1163 'Non-cash asset'

(1) In the Companies Acts 'non-cash asset' means any property or interest in property, other than cash.

For this purpose 'cash' includes foreign currency.

(2) A reference to the transfer or acquisition of a non-cash asset includes –

(a) the creation or extinction of an estate or interest in, or a right over, any property, and

(b) the discharge of a liability of any person, other than a liability for a liquidated sum.

© Crown copyright

* * *

Source 2

Encyclopaedia of Forms and Precedents, Companies, Volume 11: Acquisitions, mergers, demergers, commentary, (1) General commentary, c: Overview of company law, 3: Directors' interests

[73]

Very often some or all of the shareholders in a company involved in a takeover or company reorganisation will also be directors of the company or of its holding company. This may cause complications where the shareholders are to receive assets from, or transfer assets to, the company as part of the transaction. This complication is partly because of the provisions of Section 190 of the Companies Act 2006 which prohibits a company from disposing of a non-cash asset of the requisite value[1] to one of its directors or a director of its holding company or any person connected with such a director, unless certain formalities are complied with. It also prohibits a company from acquiring a non-cash asset of more than the requisite value from such a director or person who is connected in this way. In either case, under Section 190, the transaction is allowed provided that the arrangement is first approved by an ordinary resolution of the company or is conditional on such approval being obtained. If the director or connected person is a director of its holding company or a person connected with such a director, the arrangement must also be approved by an ordinary resolution of the members of its holding company or be conditional on such approval being obtained. Section 190 does not apply to:[2]

> a transaction between a company and a person in his character as a member of that company (eg subscription by a director for shares in the company);

> a transaction between a holding company and its wholly-owned subsidiary or between two wholly-owned subsidiaries of the same holding company;

> an arrangement entered into by a company which is being wound up (unless the winding up is by way of members' voluntary winding up) or which is in administration; or

> a transaction on a recognised investment exchange[3] effected by a director, or a person connected with him, through the agency of a person who in relation to the transaction acts as an independent broker.[4]

Any arrangement entered into by a company in contravention of Section 190 (and any transaction entered into pursuant to it) is voidable at the instance of the company unless:[5]

> it is no longer possible to restore any money or other asset which was the subject matter of the arrangement or transaction; or

> the company has been indemnified in pursuance of this section by any other person for the loss or damage suffered by it; or

20.7 the avoidance would affect rights acquired in good faith, for value and without actual notice of the contravention by a person who is not a party to the arrangement or transaction.

The company will lose the right to avoid the arrangement or any resulting transaction if the shareholders of the company (or of the holding company where appropriate) affirm it within a reasonable period.[6]

Whether or not the company has avoided the arrangement or any resulting transaction, with certain exceptions the following will be liable to account to the company for any gain which is made directly or indirectly by the arrangement or transaction:[7]

20.8 any director of the company or of its holding company;

20.9 any person with whom the company entered into the offending arrangement who is connected with a director of the company or of its holding company;

20.10 the director of the company or of its holding company with whom any person is connected; and

20.11 any other director of the company who authorised the arrangement or any transaction entered into in pursuance of that arrangement.

Subject to certain exceptions, any of the above people will also be liable (jointly and severally with any other person who is so liable) to indemnify the company for any loss or damage resulting from the arrangement or transaction.[8]

Section 190 may be of particular relevance in the situation where a new company is formed as a vehicle for the management buy-out, and that new company is connected to a director of the target company by virtue of him being a director or a shareholder.

---

[1] A non-cash asset is of the requisite value if at the time when the arrangement is entered into its value is not less than £5,000 but (subject to that) exceeds £100,000 or 10% of the company's asset value: Companies Act 2006 s 191(2).
[2] Companies Act 2006 ss 192, 193, 194.
[3] 'Recognised investment exchange' has the same meaning as in the Financial Services and Markets Act 2000 Pt 18: Companies Act 2006 s 194(2)(b).
[4] 'Independent broker' means a person who, independently of the director or any person connected with him, selects the person with whom the transaction is to be effected: Companies Act 2006 s 194(2)(a).
[5] Companies Act 2006 s 195(2).
[6] Companies Act 2006 s 196.
[7] Companies Act 2006 s 195(3)(a), (4). This is the case whether or not the arrangement is avoided by the company.
[8] Companies Act 2006 s 195(3)(b).

* * *

Source 3

Reproduced by permission of RELX (UK) Limited, trading as LexisNexis.

Gore-Browne on Companies, **Part IV Directors and management, Chapter 16 Directors' specific obligations**

Substantial property transactions entered into before 1 October 2007

[15]

Sections 320 to 322 of the Companies Act 1985 continue to apply to substantial property transactions entered into before 1 October 2007. As it is still theoretically possible for an issue to arise under these provisions, brief reference to them is retained. The substance of them is largely the same, the principal differences being as follows:

(1) the minimum value of an asset caught by s 320 is £2,000 rather than £5,000;
(2) under s 320 a company cannot enter into a contract which is conditional on member approval;
(3) there is no provision in s 320 for the aggregation of non-cash assets forming part of an arrangement or series of arrangements for the purpose of determining whether the financial thresholds have been exceeded;
(4) payments under directors' service contracts and payments for loss of office are not excluded from the requirements of ss 320 to 322; and
(5) there is no exception for transactions made by companies in administration.

* * *

Source 4

Reproduced by permission of RELX (UK) Limited, trading as LexisNexis.

Halsbury's Laws of England, Companies (Volume 14 (2023), paras 1–467; volume 14a (2023), paras 468–919; volume 15 (2023), paras 920–1445; volume 15a (2023), paras 1446–1924), 2. Companies registered under the Companies Acts, (14) Company directors, (vii) Transactions with directors requiring approval of members, d. Substantial property transactions with directors

608. Requirement of members' approval for substantial property transactions with directors.

A company[1] may not enter into an arrangement under which:[2]

> (1) a director[3] of the company or of its holding company,[4] or a person connected with such a director,[5] acquires or is to acquire[6] from the company, whether directly or indirectly, a substantial non-cash asset;[7] or ...

---

[1] As to the meaning of 'company' under the Companies Acts see PARA 25.

[2] See the Companies Act 2006 s 190(1).
As to the general application of Pt 10 Ch 4 (ss 188–225) see PARA 603.

[3] For the purposes of the Companies Act 2006 ss 190–196 (see also PARAS 609–611), a shadow director is treated as a director: s 223(1)(b). As to the meaning of 'director' see PARA 514. As to the meaning of 'shadow director' see PARA 515.
As to an application of s 190 to a shadow director see *Ultraframe (UK) Ltd v Fielding; Northstar Systems Ltd v Fielding* [2005] EWHC 1638 (Ch), [2005] All ER (D) 397 (Jul). As to how the provisions of the Companies Act 2006 Pt 10 Ch 4 interact with the directors' general duties see PARA 604.

[4] As to the meaning of 'holding company' see PARA 26.

[5] As to the meaning of references to a person being 'connected' with a director see PARA 517.
As to the validity generally of transactions involving a director or a person connected with a director see PARA 266.

[6] There is no basis for interpreting the words 'is to acquire' in the Companies Act 2006 s 190(1) as 'may acquire'; s 190(1) requires a high degree of certainty at the time when the arrangement is entered into that the asset will be acquired: *Smithton Ltd v Naggar* [2014] EWCA Civ 939, [2015] 1 WLR 189, [2015] 2 BCLC 22.

[7] Companies Act 2006 s 190(1)(a).
In the Companies Acts, 'non-cash asset' means any property or interest in property, other than cash; and, for this purpose, 'cash' includes foreign currency: s 1163(1). A reference to the transfer or acquisition of a non-cash asset includes: (1) the creation or extinction of an estate or interest in, or a right over, any property; and (2) the discharge of a liability of any person, other than a liability for a liquidated sum: see s 1163(2). In the context of the Companies Act 1985 s 739 (definition of 'non-cash asset': see now the Companies Act 2006 s 1163), an 'estate' in property means a legal or equitable estate in real property, and an 'interest' in property is something that can be defined by reference to proprietary concepts, or at least by concepts that are legally recognisable and enforceable (so that a financial or economic advantage would not qualify); 'rights over' property means legally enforceable rights: *Granada Group Ltd v Law Debenture Pension Trust Corpn plc* [2016] EWCA Civ 1289, [2017] 2 BCLC 1. As to the nature of the assets that fall within heads (1) and (2) above see also *Micro Leisure Ltd v County Properties & Developments Ltd* 1999 SC 501, 1999 SLT 1307, Ct of Sess. As to the criteria that ought to be applied when calculating the value of a non-cash asset see *Micro Leisure Ltd v County Properties and Developments Ltd (No 2)* 1999 SLT 1428 (value must be determined in the context of the particular transaction). An exclusive licence of design rights is a non-cash asset for this purpose as the ability of the licensee

to exercise rights which would otherwise be exercisable by the design right owner is a right over property: *Ultraframe (UK) Ltd v Fielding; Northstar Systems Ltd v Fielding* [2005] EWHC 1638 (Ch), [2005] All ER (D) 397 (Jul). For the purposes of the Companies Act 2006 s 190, an arrangement involving more than one non-cash asset, or an arrangement that is one of a series involving non-cash assets, must be treated as if they involved a non-cash asset of a value equal to the aggregate value of all the non-cash assets involved in the arrangement or, as the case may be, the series: see s 190(5).

The meaning of a 'substantial non-cash asset' for the purposes of s 190 is given in s 191: see ss 190(1), 191(1). Accordingly, an asset is a 'substantial' asset in relation to a company if its value: (a) exceeds 10% of the company's asset value and is more than £5,000; or (b) exceeds £100,000: see s 191(2). For this purpose, a company's 'asset value' at any time is either: (i) the value of the company's net assets determined by reference to its most recent statutory accounts; or (ii) if no statutory accounts have been prepared, the amount of the company's called-up share capital: see s 191(3). A company's 'statutory accounts' means its annual accounts prepared in accordance with Pt 15 (see PARA 1263 et seq), and its 'most recent' statutory accounts means those in relation to which the time for sending them out to members (see s 424; and PARA 1398) is most recent: s 191(4). Whether an asset is a substantial asset is to be determined as at the time the arrangement is entered into: s 191(5). The onus is on the person alleging a contravention of the provision to prove that the value of the non-cash asset exceeds the requisite value: *Niltan Carson Ltd (joint receivers and managers) v Hawthorne* [1988] BCLC 298 (decided under the Companies Act 1948 s 48(1), which governed the acquisition of 'one or more non-cash assets of the requisite value from the company'). ...

* * *

Smithton Ltd (formerly Hobart Capital Markets Ltd) v Naggar [2014] EWCA Civ 939

Arden LJ

Section 190 issue

92. The issue here is whether the judge was wrong to reject Hobart's argument that section 190 of the Companies Act 2006 was infringed when it entered into arrangements with Mr Naggar in connection with CFDs for clients who were Mr Naggar's connected persons for the purposes of that section. If this argument succeeds, those contacts were voidable and Mr Naggar is obliged to indemnify Hobart for its loss. If section 190 applies, it does so because Mr Naggar was a director of Hobart's holding company and not because Mr Naggar was a *de facto* or shadow director of Hobart.

93. As in force at the material time, section 190 provides:

    '190 Substantial property transactions: requirement of members' approval

    (1) A company may not enter into an arrangement under which –

        (a) a director of the company or of its holding company, or a person connected with such a director, acquires or is to acquire from the company (directly or indirectly) a substantial non-cash asset, or

        (b) the company acquires or is to acquire a substantial non-cash asset (directly or indirectly) from such a director or a person so connected, unless the arrangement has been approved by a resolution of the members of the company or is conditional on such approval being obtained.

For the meaning of 'substantial non-cash asset' see section 191.

(2) If the director or connected person is a director of the company's holding company or a person connected with such a director, the arrangement must also have been approved by a resolution of the members of the holding company or be conditional on such approval being obtained.'

94. The words in subsection (1) 'or is conditional on such approval being obtained' did not appear in section 190 when originally enacted. That produced the inconvenient result that arrangements could not be made conditionally on shareholder approval subsequently being obtained.

95. As Lewison J held in *Ultraframe (UK) Ltd v Fielding* [2005] EWHC 1638 Ch [1392], with respect to the predecessor section (section 320 of the Companies Act 1985), the question whether an arrangement falls within the section must be asked on the basis of the arrangement as at its inception.

96. It is not said that the CFDs were non-cash assets of the requisite value but that the shares by which they were referenced were 'substantial non-cash assets' as those expressions are defined for the purposes of section 190: see CA 2006, sections 191(2) and 1163(1).

Submissions on this appeal

Appellant's submissions

103. Mr Marshall focuses in his oral submissions on the wider basis. He submits that section 190 should be interpreted so as to cast the net widely in order to achieve its statutory purpose and that the fact that it covers conditional arrangements shows that the judge was wrong to hold that a high degree of certainty is required.

104. Mr Marshall submits that section 190 is engaged if there was a real prospect that the connected person would opt to take the shares on closing out. If so, where Hobart was the CFD provider, the shares would be sold to Hobart and Hobart would on sell them to the CFD holder who would be Mr Naggar or one of his connected persons. In practice, submits Mr Marshall, Mr Naggar and his connected companies had worked to build up a stake in F & C and thereby to encourage takeover activity so it was likely that they would exercise their option to take the physical referenced shares.

105. Mr Marshall relies on *Re Duckwari plc* [1999] Ch 253 where a company bought the right to complete a contract for the purchase of a property from a company which was a connected person of one of its directors and this court heard an appeal as to the amount of the director's statutory liability. Mr Marshall makes the point that, under that arrangement, there was clearly no requirement for the company to acquire the property if it did not wish to do so (see, per Nourse LJ, at pp 259–260). In my judgment, that case does not assist Mr Marshall because the right was itself a non-cash asset of the requisite value. This may be seen from the earlier decision in *Re Duckwari plc (No 1)* [1997] 2 BCLC 713, in which this court held that the statutory predecessor of section 190 applied to that arrangement. In the present case, Hobart does not contend that the CFDs were non-cash assets of the requisite value.

106. Mr Michael Crystal QC presented the case for Mr Naggar on the section 190 issue. It is not necessary to deal with all of his submissions. On the wider basis, Mr Crystal submits that the CFD holder had no legal entitlement to the referenced shares but the judge held that in practice he would have been allowed to take them should he wish to do so. However, Mr Crystal also submits that it was not certain that the CFD holder would be able to fund the purchase:

the purchase of the referenced shares when the CFDs were finally closed out would have required some £151m. The effect of the words 'is to acquire' is that until Mr Naggar decided to acquire the referenced shares it cannot be said that he entered into an arrangement which met the requirements of the section. On his submission there has to be an objective manifestation of an intention for the acquisition of an asset. Otherwise the arrangement is not within the section.

107. As to the narrower basis, Mr Marshall's written submissions contended that Dr May's evidence supporting the finding of a rule or practice was plainly a wrong interpretation of the relevant rule on waivers from the riskless principal rule. Mr Crystal relied on the judge's finding and other points.

108. In my judgment, the appeal should be dismissed on both the wider and the narrower basis.

109. As to the narrower basis, the argument turns on the fact that a purchaser was not identified until the end of the day on which the shares were purchased. But by the end of the day the purchaser was ascertained and therefore its acquisition of the shares operated with effect from the earliest moment in the day under the law of ratification. So in the end the CFD provider acquired shares and ratified the purchase and section 190 was never on this basis engaged. Furthermore, the judge found as a fact that Hobart would in those circumstances be treated under the rules of the market as not having acquired any interest, and there has been no effective challenge to that finding.

110. As to the wider basis, in my judgment the judge was correct in her conclusion. It is only necessary to focus on one point. Section 190 requires an arrangement (which can be a non-contractual arrangement) under which a director or connected person acquires 'or is to acquire' an interest in shares. There is no basis for interpreting the words 'is to acquire' as 'may acquire'. The fact that conditional arrangements are permitted does not require this interpretation since even a conditional arrangement must still satisfy the words quoted even if it is conditional. Since, when the arrangement was made for the CFDs to be written there was no certainty that on closing out the CFD holder would opt to acquire the referenced shares, section 190 does not apply. The arrangement was not said to be made on closing out and election to take the referenced shares.

Conclusion

111. I would dismiss the appeal on both issues raised on this appeal. The judge held that Mr Naggar was not a *de facto* or shadow director of Hobart and there is no basis for setting aside that finding on this appeal. The claim by Hobart against Mr Naggar under Companies Act 2006, section 190 for indemnification on the grounds that the arrangements between him and Hobart for the acquisition of F&C shares to be used to hedge CFDs fails because (1) the technical grounds for saying that an acquisition by Hobart of an interest in shares occurred in the course of purchase fail in law and on the evidence, and (2) the arrangements themselves provided only a means whereby the CFD holders *might* ultimately acquire non-cash assets of the requisite value, namely shares by which the contracts for differences were referenced, not that they would do so.

*   *   *

Source 6

Reproduced by permission of RELX (UK) Limited, trading as LexisNexis.

Tolley's Company Law Handbook, Chapter 18 Directors

Is an indemnity agreement a substantial property transaction? The High Court, in *Terry v Watchstone Ltd [2018] EWHC 3082*, had to determine, among other things, whether an indemnity agreement was a substantial property transaction under *CA 2006, s 190*.

M plc had acquired the entire issued share capital of W Ltd under an SPA. Before execution of the SPA, W had agreed to fully indemnify the seller shareholders (who were one of W's directors and persons connected with him) for both tax liabilities (excluding capital gains tax on the ultimate disposal of shares) and other liabilities and costs they might incur as a consequence of the sale. W later challenged the indemnity, arguing that it was a substantial property transaction which, wrongly W said, had not been approved by shareholders.

The court held that the indemnity was *not* a 'non-cash asset' within *CA 2006, ss 190* and *1163*. This was because the indemnity did not constitute 'property' or 'interest in property': those words did not include everything other than cash. The rights granted by the indemnity were no more than non-marketable contractual rights. They were merely rights to receive cash payments if certain events occurred.

The court also held that the indemnity was not an asset acquired by the sellers because it could not be said it had been in existence immediately prior to the acquisition. Rather, the rights granted by the indemnity had been brought into existence by the grant itself; there was no acquisition of pre-existing rights. Moreover, the indemnity had been acquired by each seller in their 'character as a member' within s *192(a)* (which provides that no approval is required for transactions between a company and a person in his character as a member of that company). The indemnity related directly to liability which each member might incur in his/her capacity as a member. Moreover, a vote had been taken on behalf of the shareholders to approve the granting of the indemnity, and those representing over 77% of shares had given approval in accordance with W's articles.

So in short, an indemnity agreement was held not to be a substantial property transaction under *CA 2006, s 190*.

An appeal in this case had been scheduled to be heard in November 2019, but a confidential commercial settlement of the dispute is understood to have been reached in October 2019.

Listed companies. In addition to the requirements of *CA 2006*, listed companies must also comply with the requirements of the Listing Rules on related party transactions. See 33.40 PUBLIC AND LISTED COMPANIES.

Charitable companies. Where a company is a charity in England and Wales, any approval given by the members of the company for the above purposes is ineffective without the prior written permission of the Charity Commission. Such written permission is also required where the payment would require approval but for the exemption on the part of the members of a body corporate that is a wholly-owned subsidiary of another body corporate.

[*Charities Act 2011, ss 201, 202; CA 2006, s 226*].

* * *

■ YOUR TURN

Have a go at answering question 2, remembering the guidance on pages 19–20.
- Create a list of the relevant legal points raised by the question.
- Create a list of the relevant answers to the legal points provided in the sources and information, remembering to use primary sources over secondary wherever possible.
- Timings are important: you will need to prepare and write your answer in one hour.

SQE1 Functioning legal knowledge link
Remember from chapter 4 of *Revise SQE: Business Law and Practice* that the powers of directors are set out in the company's articles. The Companies Act (CA) 2006 sets out a number of restrictions on directors including s 190 CA 2006, which requires substantial property transactions to be subject to shareholders' approval by OR.

EVALUATING YOUR ANSWER

When you have attempted question 2, mark it yourself against the SQE2 legal research assessment criteria. Do you think your attempt met the threshold standard?

Now compare your attempt with the following key legal points and the sample answers to question 2. A circled number indicates that commentary is provided for this part of the answer. The commentary will explain whether or not the sample is likely to meet the threshold SQE2 standard.

➡Key legal points: Question 2

Note, references to CA 2006 are references to the Companies Act 2006.

In this assessment, part, or all, of the following sources are relevant to the question:

- Companies Act 2006 ss 190, 191, 252, 253, 1163
- *Halsbury's Laws of England*, Companies, Vol. 14a, para 608
- *Smithton Ltd (formerly Hobart Capital Markets Ltd) v Naggar* [2014] EWCA Civ 939.

The following sources are not relevant to the question:

- *Encyclopaedia of Forms and Precedents*, Vol. 11(1)c, 3 Directors' interests
- *Gore-Browne on Companies*, Part IV Directors and management, Chapter 16 Directors' specific obligations
- *Tolley's Company Law Handbook*, Chapter 18 Directors.

While the reference to *Halsbury's Laws* is relevant to answering the question, it summarises the position that is set out in *Smithton* and the highlighted statutory provisions. Where the primary sources are provided in addition to a commentary on those sources, you should rely on those primary sources, not secondary sources such as *Halsbury's*.

Key legal points:

- Under s 190 CA 2006, a company may not enter into an arrangement under which a director or a person connected with a director acquires or is to acquire from the company (directly or indirectly) a substantial non-cash asset. This is the case unless the arrangement has been approved by the company's shareholders, or is conditional on such approval being obtained.

- A director's father is considered a family member connected with a director (ss 252, 253 CA 2006).
- A substantial non-cash asset is an asset that is more than £5,000 and over 10% of the company's net assets, or that is over £100,000 (s 191 CA 2006) and is not cash (s 1163 CA 2006).
- The shares by which the contracts for difference (CFDs) were referenced could be substantial non-cash assets (s 1163 CA 2006).
- Section 190(1) requires that at the time the transaction is entered into, there is a high degree of certainty that the asset will be acquired, according to the case of *Smithton Ltd (formerly Hobart Capital Markets Ltd) v Naggar* [2014].
- In *Smithton Ltd*, it was held that when the arrangement was made for the CFDs to be written, there was no certainty that on closing out the CFD holder would opt to acquire the referenced shares, and therefore s 190 CA did not apply. The arrangement provided only a means whereby the CFD holders *might* ultimately acquire the relevant shares, not that they would do so.

■ SAMPLE ANSWER 1 TO QUESTION 2

Sangita is a director of Chabler Ltd ('Chabler'). Chabler wrote Sangita's father a contract for difference ('CFD') which is an arrangement under which Sangita's father might acquire shares in Matters on the closed out date, which is an unspecified date in the next six months. ❶

I have researched whether Sangita needs to obtain shareholders' approval if her father buys shares in Matters at the closed out date. ❷

Sangita is a director of Chabler. Under s 190(1) Companies Act 2006 (CA 2006) a company may not enter into an arrangement under which a person connected with a director acquires from the company a substantial non-cash asset without shareholders' approval. ❸ Sangita's father would be considered a person connected with her, a director according to ss 252 and 253 CA 2006. ❹

Arden LJ in *Smithton Ltd (formerly Hobart Capital Markets Ltd) v Naggar* [2014] EWCA Civ 939 stated that 'when the arrangement was made for the CFDs to be written there was no certainty that on closing out the CFD holder would opt to acquire the referenced shares, section 190 does not apply'. ❺

The arrangement between Chabler and Sangita's father is not a definitive arrangement to acquire shares in Matters from Chabler. Sangita's father might not choose to purchase the shares on the closed out date and there is no obligation on him to do so. It is therefore likely that s 190 CA 2006 will not apply to Chabler's CFD contract with Sangita's father. ❻

In addition, according to s 191(2) CA 2006, 'An asset is a substantial asset in relation to a company if its value (a) exceeds 10% of the company's asset value and is more than £5,000, or (b) exceeds £100,000'. Section 1163 CA 2006 states 'a non-cash asset means any property or interest in property, other than cash'. The CFDs are not substantial non-cash assets, as there is no commitment to buy the shares in Matters. If shares in Matters were acquired, they might be considered a substantial non-cash asset (ss 191(2), 1163(1) CA 2006). ❼

Based on the case of *Smithton*, it is unlikely that s 190 CA 2006 will apply to the arrangement between Chabler and Sangita's father for the CFD to be written. Consequently, no shareholders' approval will be required for the CFD. ❽

COMMENTARY

❶ This opening paragraph provides a little background and context to the client's question, setting out the relevant facts: the relationship between Sangita, Chabler and Sangita's father, details of what is meant by a CFD, and the timeframe for any purchase of shares in Matters.

❷ This sets out the question the client is seeking an answer to, linking it to the relevant facts.

❸ The primary source being the Companies Act 2006 is correctly identified, and the relevant section is introduced and explained in a client-focused manner.

❹ The relevant sections of the Companies Act have been identified and extracted. The role of Sangita and her father, and how they are considered connected in accordance with s 253 CA 2006, are clearly set out in a client-friendly manner, demonstrating correct application of the law to the client's situation.

❺ Case law assists in the interpretation of statute. A large extract of the judgment was provided in the bundle and the relevant material has been identified and extracted.

❻ The relevant law has been explained and is then correctly applied to the client's situation. An explanation as to why s 190 CA 2006 would not apply is provided, using clear, precise, concise and acceptable language.

❼ Again, the relevant law has been identified and extracted. Key information from the facts is also extracted (that there was no obligation on any client to buy the shares in Matters) and the relevant legal principle is then applied. Note how names are used rather than generic terms, which enables the advice to be clear and client-focused.

❽ A final sentence answering the client's question ensures the advice is client-focused and addresses the client's problem.

Does this answer meet the threshold?

When assessing the first report against the SQE2 legal research assessment criteria, it is likely that this would meet the threshold standard for the SQE2 legal research assessment. The candidate selected the correct sources for this question and disregarded the irrelevant sources. The relevant law was identified from the sources and applied correctly and comprehensively to the client's situation, and the language throughout is clear, precise, concise and acceptable.

Now consider the second sample answer to question 2.

■ SAMPLE ANSWER 2 TO QUESTION 2

Sangita Shah is the managing director of Chabler Ltd, a company that was incorporated a few years ago. She holds 45% of the shares in Chabler, with two other shareholders, Punit Sharma and Jinka Wu who hold 30% and 25% of the shares respectively. Chabler provides the full range of brokering services to investors, including the creation of 'long and short contracts for difference'. Felicity Crawford and Roland Rames are the other company directors. ❶

Sangita would need shareholders' approval if her father buys shares in Matters at the closed out date. ❷

Sangita is the managing director and majority shareholder of Chablers Ltd, a company that provides the full range of brokering services to investors, including the creation of 'long and short contracts for difference'. The other two shareholders are Punit Sharma and Jinka Wu who hold 30% and 25% of the shares respectively. The other directors are Felicity Crawford and Roland Rames. ❸

Chabler wrote contracts for differences for shares in Matters on behalf of Chabler's clients who included Sangita's father. ❹ There was no fixed closing out date in the contracts for differences.

As Sangita's father is connected with Sangita who is a director of Chabler, no transactions can be entered into between Chabler and Sangita's father without shareholders' prior approval, in accordance with s 190 CA 2006. ❺

If Sangita's dad decides to acquire shares in Matters at the closing out date, Chabler will have to transfer those shares from itself to him. This will then fall within s 190 CA 2006 as Sangita's father will be acquiring the shares in Matters from Chabler. ❻

An ordinary resolution of the shareholders of Chabler would be required to approve the transaction for Sangita's father to buy the shares in Matters, ❼ otherwise the transaction would be voidable at the instance of the company (s 195 CA 2006). ❽

COMMENTARY

❶ This text just restates the introductory paragraph from the partner, containing lots of information that is not relevant to answering the client's question. It is important to extract only the relevant facts when writing the answer.

❷ This is client-focused advice which answers the client's question, but the advice is incorrect and no context is provided in relation to the client's situation. Sangita does not need to obtain shareholders' approval as demonstrated in the case of *Smithton*. See point 5 below.

❸ This paragraph simply restates the facts and repeats the first paragraph of the instructions, without extracting just the relevant information. It is important to be clear, precise and concise in the answer, and identify and include only what is relevant information to answer the client's question. The candidate also refers to 'Chablers Ltd', which is not the correct name of the business: it is Chabler Ltd.

❹ There is no explanation of what is meant by a contract for difference. It would have been helpful to set out what such a contract entails. Also a contract for difference could have been defined as 'CFD' or similar, to assist with the use of clear, precise and acceptable language.

❺ Section 190 CA 2006 is the key statutory provision relevant for this question so the relevant primary source has been correctly identified. However, the terms used in this section which are referred to elsewhere in the sources (eg ss 191(2), 252, 253, 1163) should have also been considered in the application of the law to the facts. The law is incorrectly applied. A company can enter into a transaction with someone who is connected with a director without shareholder approval in some instances – for example, where it does not involve a 'substantial non-cash asset'. There is no explanation as to why Sangita's father is connected with Sangita, demonstrating a failure to provide client-focused advice and apply the law comprehensively to the client's situation.

❻ Again, this is not correct. The *Smithton* case in Arden LJ's judgment at paragraph 109 states that under a CFD, a purchaser for the shares is not identified until the end of the day on which the shares are purchased. Under the law of ratification, the shares are deemed acquired at the earliest moment of the day. These shares would be acquired by Sangita's father directly from Matters, rather than from Chabler, so s 190 CA 2006 would not be applicable. Note also the colloquial language in the answer, using 'dad' instead of 'father'; this is not appropriate language.

❼ This is an incorrect conclusion reached from the law provided, although it is expressed in a way that is client-focused.

⑧ The client did not ask what action might be taken if shareholders' approval was not obtained, so s 195 CA 2006 is not relevant. While it is commendable to anticipate and address related issues, it is important to focus primarily on the question asked.

Does this answer meet the threshold?

When assessing the second report against the SQE2 legal research assessment criteria, it is unlikely that this would meet the threshold standard. No reference is made to the *Smithton* case despite it being provided. It was a relevant source as it elaborated on the application of s 190 to uncertain arrangements. Several items of relevant law were overlooked and not included, despite being integral to the application of s 190 to uncertain arrangements. This resulted in the report failing to apply the law correctly and comprehensively to the client's situation.

■ KEY POINT CHECKLIST

This chapter has covered the following key knowledge points:
• The SQE2 assessment criteria for legal research and applying them in the context of business organisations, rules and procedures.
• A suggested structure for approaching an SQE2 legal research question.
• Sample answers which would be either likely or unlikely to meet the threshold standard, with full commentary on their strengths and weaknesses.

■ SUMMARY AND REFLECTION

In order to succeed in the SQE2 legal research assessment, think carefully about what the question is asking you, read the documentation thoroughly and consider the relevance of the sources provided to answer your question. You will need to make quick decisions on which to discard and which to use in your answer.

SQE2 assesses your ability to apply the law both correctly *and* comprehensively so it is really important that you consider the relevant law and explain how it is applicable to the wider context of the client's scenario, as well as to the more obvious narrow points.

Your report should be written in client-friendly language without using too much legal jargon or legalistic terms. Practise clear writing with appropriate explanations of the law so that the client will be able to understand the advice given to them and your legal justification for this advice.

Now take the time to reflect and consider what you might still need to work on, and whether you feel completely confident in your legal research skills in the context of business organisations, rules and procedures.

3

Legal writing

■ MAKE SURE YOU KNOW

This chapter covers the skill of legal writing in the context of business organisations, rules and procedures. Legal writing in this area is one of the skills that will be assessed on day three of the SQE2 written skills assessments (see the Introduction for more detail). You must consider who your client is and who your writing is directed towards. For example, if your client is a company and the recipient of your letter/email is one of the directors, you should be mindful of whether any content should be kept confidential and not disclosed to any of the other director(s). The same issue may apply to partnerships.

As with the other written skills assessments, remember that your knowledge of legal principles and practices associated with business organisations, business taxation, money laundering and financial services will be tested, as well as the application of contract law to these principles. We therefore recommend that you read this revision guide once you are familiar with the contents of ***Revise SQE: Business Law and Practice*** and ***Revise SQE: Contract Law***.

This chapter provides examples of how different scenarios relating to business organisations, rules and procedures, taxation for businesses, money laundering and financial services could arise in the context of a SQE2 legal writing assessment.

■ SQE ASSESSMENT ADVICE

As you work through this chapter, remember to pay particular attention in your revision to:
- the inclusion of relevant facts in the sample answers
- the way in which letters and emails are structured and how this could be applied generally
- the ways in which the advice given is tailored to the client/recipient and the information you are given about them in the sample questions
- how the sample answers use clear and concise language
- how the law is applied to the client's situation
- the way in which any ethical or professional conduct issues are identified and resolved.

See the Appendix for the SRA's performance indicators in legal writing.

■ INTRODUCTION TO LEGAL WRITING IN BUSINESS ORGANISATIONS, RULES AND PROCEDURES

The SQE2 assessment usually includes scenarios which occur in day-to-day legal practice. A key aspect of practising in the field of business organisations, rules and procedures is the ability to follow advice given by a solicitor to a client after a meeting or over the telephone with a clearly articulated written communication. Your SQE2 assessment in legal writing will be based on reading a memo or email from a partner which asks you to provide advice to a client. This will usually follow a fictitious telephone call or meeting which has taken place between the partner and the client. The question will give you some direction about the areas you need to cover in your letter or email, but you will need to apply your knowledge of those areas to the scenario and communicate the relevant advice to the client clearly and concisely in writing. This chapter will provide examples of how you can do this and meet the criteria for the SQE2 legal writing assessment at the same time.

The key to success in your SQE2 legal writing assessment is approaching the question in a structured manner. Try adopting the following approach:

1. Once you have read the question, write down the key legal and procedural points that you feel need to be communicated to the client.
2. You can then form the structure of the letter or email you are asked to write around those key legal points by using headings or subheadings.
3. Write your answer.
4. Review your answer, keeping in mind the SQE2 legal writing assessment criteria.

Assessment technique

When reviewing your answer, read the draft and ask yourself whether or not it answers the client's question(s) clearly and concisely. Avoid using long sentences and overly technical language, and plan the structure of your letter or email based around what you have been asked to consider.

SQE2 legal writing assessment criteria

Try to remember these points as you construct your answer:

Skills

1. Include relevant facts.
2. Use a logical structure.
3. Advice/content is client- and recipient-focused.
4. Use clear, precise, concise and acceptable language which is appropriate to the recipient.

Application of law

5. Apply the law correctly to the client's situation.
6. Apply the law comprehensively to the client's situation, identifying any ethical and professional conduct issues and exercising judgement to resolve them honestly and with integrity.

In chapter 1 of **Revise SQE: Business Law and Practice**, we considered the different options for forming a business. Question 1 below demonstrates how your knowledge of this topic could be tested in the context and format of a SQE2 legal writing assessment.

■ QUESTION 1

Email to candidate

From: Partner
Sent: 1 May 202#
To: Candidate
Subject: Business development

I am acting for Grace Olancey who occasionally sells various handmade crochet shawls at local craft markets. Grace was recently approached by Jacinta Arkwright, the owner of Crochet By Hand, a boutique based in Chelsea who would like to sell her shawls in her shops.

Grace is very keen to have her items in a physical shop, particularly one such as Crochet By Hand as she no longer enjoys the market day experience, especially when the weather is wet and she has to work at the stall all day. Jacinta seemed to think that Grace's shawls would fly off the shelves in her shop and she could charge a hefty premium, significantly more than she receives from her market sales. Jacinta has provided draft Heads of Terms setting out the key provisions that have been agreed between Grace and Jacinta, which I have attached (Attachment 1).

When Grace telephoned me she was very excited about Jacinta's proposal, as she thinks other small boutique stores might offer similar deals. Grace sought advice on setting up a business to sell the shawls and we discussed the possibility of her incorporating a company – 'Graces Ltd' – through which to sell her shawls. Grace mentioned that she has substantial savings set aside for her daughter's education. I ran through the differences between operating as a sole trader and a company, and said I would set this out in a letter for her to review.

Unfortunately, I have been called to deal with another urgent matter, so I need you to write the letter for me.

I would like you to explain to Grace Olancey:

- **the ownership, management and liability differences between a company as compared with a sole trader**
- **any registration or other formalities that she should be aware of**
- **how Grace's tax treatment might be affected if she opted to trade as a company.**

Grace is not a lawyer, so it is important that your explanation is clear and simple. You should be aware that Grace is very intelligent and curious, wanting to understand everything, so you will need to provide brief explanations where appropriate.

Thanks

Partner

Note to candidates:

Please assume that all issues in relation to client care/money laundering have already been dealt with by the partner.

Attachment 1

DRAFT Heads of Terms:
These Heads of Terms set out the key terms of agreement
BETWEEN

Crochet By Hand Ltd, whose registered office is Fulmers LLP, Chelsea House, Fulham Road SW16 3LP (company number X493321) ('CBH')

Grace Olancey of 15 Dreams Close, Dartford RM20 3SR ('Grace')

1. Supply
   Grace to supply 10 units of 150 cm x 100 cm handmade woollen crocheted scarves to CBH per month.

2. Price:
   CBH to make the scarves available for sale to the public in the retail shop at a minimum price of £35 + VAT per unit, unless otherwise agreed between CBH and Grace.

3. Payment:
    CBH to pay Grace 60% of any sales proceeds received from the sale of Grace's
    scarves to the public.

4. Term:
    Trial for three months commencing on [1 April 202#]

* * *

■ YOUR TURN

Have a go at answering question 1, remembering the guidance on pages 57–58.
*   Refer to the structured approach in the SRA's assessment criteria on page 58.
*   Create a list of the most salient legal points raised by the question.
*   Timings are important: you will need to prepare and write your answer in 30 minutes.

SQE1 Functioning legal knowledge link

Remember from chapter 1 of *Revise SQE: Business Law and Practice* that a company
as an incorporated business will have its own legal identity and its liability limited
shares, and will need to be registered with Companies House. There is no legal
distinction between a sole trader and its owner/manager. The liability of a sole trader
is unlimited.

EVALUATING YOUR ANSWER

When you have attempted question 1, mark it yourself against the SQE2 legal writing
assessment criteria. Do you think your attempt met the threshold standard?

Now compare your attempt with the following key legal points and two sample answers
to question 1. A circled number indicates that commentary is provided for this part of
the answer. The commentary will explain whether or not the sample is likely to meet the
threshold SQE2 standard.

➡ Key legal points: Question 1

*   A sole trader is a self-employed person who is the sole owner and who runs their
    business. A company is a person separate from its shareholders and directors.
    Directors run a company; shareholders own shares in the company.
*   The liability of a sole trader is unlimited. The business owner is personally and
    directly responsible for all debts and liabilities incurred by the business, so the
    owner's personal assets might be at risk. The liability of the owners of a company
    that is limited by shares (i.e. the shareholders) is capped to the amount they have
    agreed to pay for the shares. Owners' personal assets are not at risk.
*   There are generally no formal requirements or legal processes required to set up
    the business of a sole trader, other than the requirement to register with HMRC.
    Companies have ongoing formalities, decision-making, filing and disclosure
    requirements.
*   A sole trader might be required to register for VAT, but otherwise any profit
    received from the business would be taxed as the business owners' income and
    subject to income tax. Companies pay corporation tax on both their income profits
    and their capital gains.

■ SAMPLE ANSWER 1 TO QUESTION 1

[*The law firm's address and contact details*]

15 Dreams Close
Dartford
RM20 3SR

1 May 202#

Dear Grace

Sole traders and companies

I refer to our recent telephone conversation in which we discussed the two trading options available to you to sell your shawls:

    a) sole trader; and
    b) company. ❶

I have set out below the key differences relating to the:

- ownership, management and liability
- registration and other formalities; and
- tax treatment

of the two different alternative business media options for you to consider. ❷

1. Sole trader ❸

A 'sole trader' is self-employed and runs their own business.

Ownership and management

There is no distinction between the business and its owners and managers for a sole trader. You would be the owner and the manager of the business. ❹

Liability

There is no legal separation between your liability and the liability of the sole trader. So you, as the business owner, would be personally and directly responsible for all debts and liabilities incurred. Any personal assets you may have, including the savings set aside for your daughter's education, even if not used in your shawl business, will be at risk if you are unable to satisfy the debts of your business. This could have the serious consequence of resulting in your bankruptcy. ❺

Registration and other formalities

There are no specific formalities or legal processes required to set up the business. However, as a sole trader, you will be self-employed and need to register with HMRC.

Tax treatment

You may be required to register for VAT if your sales exceed a certain threshold, which is currently over £85,000. As a sole trader, you would pay income tax on your business' trading profits and capital gains tax on its capital gains.

2. Graces Ltd

We spoke about incorporating Graces Ltd as a private company, limited by shares with you being the only shareholder and the only director.

Ownership and management

Companies are separate legal entities, which means that they can own property, enter into contracts, owe money, etc, even though it will be you making the shawls and other products to generate the sales. So Graces Ltd, and not you personally, would enter into a contract with Crochet By Hand for the supply of shawls.

Shareholders own shares in the company, while directors have general management powers to run the company on a day-to-day basis. You would assume both these roles (which is often the case for small businesses) but you should note that they are separate and distinct roles in law.

Liability

The company's liability would be limited to value of the shares. So, if Graces Ltd was incorporated with 100 shares of £1 each, and you were the only shareholder, you would invest £100 in the company from the outset. Your personal liability to contribute towards the debts of Graces Ltd would then be capped at that £100. If Graces Ltd was wound up, you would have no further liability as you would already have fully paid the shares. Your daughter's education fund would not be impacted. For smaller businesses, this separation of liability is one of the main benefits of being a company.

Registration/formalities

There are some formalities and reporting requirements that companies must comply with, with which the firm would be happy to help. ❻ For example:

- Every company must be registered with Companies House, and certain information about the company will be freely accessible to the public.
- A company must have a registered office, which is an address to which all formal notices can be sent. This firm serves as a registered office for many of our client companies, and can provide this service to Graces Ltd.
- Every company must have at least one director. This is a person who has management responsibility for the company and as stated above, I assume you would want this role. ❼

The company must comply with other ongoing formality, decision-making, filing and disclosure requirements, with which the firm can assist you.

Tax treatment

Companies pay corporation tax on both their income profits and their capital gains. This is separate to any income tax you might pay in your personal capacity.

Conclusion

The benefits of limited liability may be significant for a small business such as yours, particularly if you want to keep your personal assets (including the savings for your daughter's education) separate from those of your business. However, you should be aware that there are costs, administrative burdens and disclosure requirements associated with setting up and running a limited company. ❽

I would be happy to assist with whichever option you choose and look forward to receiving your further information.

Yours sincerely

Partner

COMMENTARY

❶ The introductory paragraph sets out the purpose of the letter. If you consider this from the perspective of a non-legally trained client, it explains why the candidate is writing to them and what information they will be able to learn from reading this letter.

❷ Note how this explicitly refers to the information that was set out in the instructions, ensuring only relevant facts are included.

3 The letter is split into two paragraphs, 1 and 2, each addressing the alternative business medium. This provides a logical structure to the letter, enabling it to be clear and recipient-focused.

4 The legal position is stated in the first sentence under the heading 'Ownership and management'. An explanation is then provided by stating how the law would apply to the client's situation. By providing this illustration and using 'you' instead of 'the sole trader', the letter is made more recipient-focused, and uses language appropriate for the recipient, who is not a lawyer.

5 The approach adopted in point 4 above is applied to all the subsequent paragraphs: stating the law and then providing an example of how it would apply to the client. Here the letter expressly refers to the client's savings, using clear, precise, concise, acceptable and appropriate language.

6 Where appropriate in the letter, reference is made to the ability of the firm to provide additional support. This demonstrates to the examiner that the candidate is aware that additional formalities and requirements exist, which might go beyond the scope of this letter, but that they would be addressed by the firm if the client chose to pursue running the business through a company. It shows that the candidate is applying the law correctly and comprehensively to the client's situation.

7 Note the use of bullet points to assist with the clarity of the structure and the provision of comprehensive advice to the client. Only a few examples are provided here, to provide the client with a broad understanding of the type of formalities and requirements a company might be subject to. This shows to the examiner that the candidate understands the client's situation and is applying the relevant law or principles to the situation.

8 The letter concludes with a brief summary of the positives of setting up a company, while highlighting the drawbacks insofar as they relate to the client's concerns. This demonstrates a client-focused approach.

Does this answer meet the threshold?

The sample answer above contains all of the information that the client requires and that the candidate has been asked to provide. It is therefore likely to meet the threshold standard for the SQE2 legal writing assessment. The answer covers all aspects of the assessment criteria for legal writing. The relevant facts are used and the law applied correctly and comprehensively to the client's situation. The logical structure adopted in the letter and the use of headings and bullet points assist in providing clear and recipient-focused advice. Remember to bear in mind the assessment criteria as you form your answer so that you address all of the SRA's requirements.

Now consider the second sample answer to question 1.

■ SAMPLE ANSWER 2 TO QUESTION 1

[The law firm's address and contact details]

15 Dreams Close
Dartford
RM20 3SR

1 May 202#

Dear Ms Olancey **1**

Your business

I refer with great enthusiasm and excitement to the telephone conversation we had yesterday and set out below a summary of our discussion. **2**

There are many differences between companies and sole traders. The key ones are: ❸

1.   Shareholders own shares in a company; collectively the shareholders 'own' the company. Shares could be ordinary shares or preference shares. ❹ Sole traders are owned by the individual running the business.
2.   Companies are artificial, separate legal entities run by the directors. Sole traders are not separate from the person who runs the business. ❺
3.   A company's liability is limited to its share capital. A sole trader's liability is uncapped and can, in the worst case scenario, result in the bankruptcy of the individual running the business. ❻
4.   Companies need to be registered at Companies House. They will receive a certificate of incorporation, which is like a company's birth certificate, and a company registration number with which it can be identified at Companies House. ❼ In addition, a company must submit annual reports, copies of shareholders' resolutions, various forms and other documents to Companies House at key times. There is no register for sole traders.
5.   Companies pay a tax specific to them known as corporation tax. Any profits of an income or a capital nature that a company makes will be subject to corporation tax. A sole trader, just like a partner in a partnership, ❽ pays income tax on the profits it generates.

On balance, I think operating as a sole trader would be the most appropriate option for you. ❾

Do call me if you would like to discuss any of the above further.

Yours sincerely

Partner

COMMENTARY

❶ The instructions referred to Grace rather than Ms Olancey, so the letter should follow that lead and be addressed to Grace, rather than Ms Olancey.

❷ The heading and the opening paragraph provide no guidance as to what is to follow in the letter. They are neither clear, precise nor concise. The introductory paragraph should set out the purpose of the letter – why the candidate is writing it and what information it contains/what questions it answers.

❸ While the letter does consider and set out the differences between companies and sole traders, the advice provided is very brief. More client- and recipient-focused advice could have been provided in relation to each of the paragraphs 1–5, to apply the law correctly to the client's situation in a way which is user-friendly, helpful and clear to the client.

❹ The reference to ordinary or preference shares is unnecessary and might confuse the client, particularly as no further explanation is given.

❺ While this correctly states the legal principle, it does not explain how that principle would apply to the client. It is important to provide the advice in context to ensure that it is client-focused.

❻ As with point 4 above, this states the principle, but does not apply the law to the client's situation. What does it mean to the client if the company's liability is limited to the share capital? There is no reference or consideration given to the client's sizeable savings put aside for her daughter's education. This would be an example of needing to include and address the relevant facts, and apply the law to the client's situation.

7 Information about the certificate of incorporation and the company's registration number is not really relevant. It does not address the client's instructions. The next sentence incorrectly states that all shareholders' resolutions need to be submitted to Companies House, so the law is not correctly applied to the client's situation.

8 The reference to partners in a partnership is irrelevant and unnecessary. It might also confuse a client.

9 The decision to operate as a sole trader appears to have been made without a clear analysis of the client's considerations.

Does this answer meet the threshold?

When assessing the second letter against the SQE2 legal writing assessment criteria, it is unlikely that this letter would meet the threshold standard for the SQE2 legal writing assessment. While this letter does address some of the key points asked for in the instructions, it fails to provide the advice in a clear and recipient-focused manner. It does not include the relevant facts, but includes several irrelevant facts, and does not apply the law correctly to the client's situation. Remember to bear in mind the assessment criteria as you form your answer so that you address all of the SRA's requirements.

As you know, SQE2 can assess any of the areas on the SQE1 Business Law and Practice specification. Below is another example of how a different part of the specification could arise in the context of legal writing on SQE2.

■ QUESTION 2

Email to candidate

From: Partner
Sent: 1 June 202#
To: Candidate
Subject: Expansion of Poppy's Pots Ltd (The Haven, Swan Lane, Hastings TN34 9LT)

We've been acting for Poppy's Pots Ltd ('PPL') for some years. We helped set up the company and the firm is PPL's registered office. PPL makes and sells a range of handmade, hand-painted outdoor plant pots. It has been developing its product range and now has a selection of pots to cater for indoor plants that are proving very popular for city offices. The outdoor pots are popular with many stately homes.

Tunde Belucchi is the Managing Director of PPL. He just telephoned me to say he thinks now is a good time for PPL to acquire its own office space with a bespoke showroom. To date, PPL has been exhibiting its products from Tunde's garden office site in Hastings. Tunde is looking at various locations in the south-east of England.

PPL currently has a business mortgage from the Bank of Hastings (the 'Bank') in respect of the garden office in Hastings. There is £200,000 outstanding on this mortgage and PPL has never missed a payment. The Bank also has a floating charge over PPL's stock. Tunde thinks the floating charge was registered with Companies House back in February 2020.

PPL has received a loan offer from Jellogs Bank plc for £740,000 for the purchase of the new office space and showroom, subject to a fixed charge over those premises and a floating charge over PPL's stock.

I explained to Tunde the different types of security available for loans, what happens when both banks have floating charges over the same assets and the purpose of registering charges.

Please could you write a letter to Tunde, explaining:

1. **the difference between a mortgage, fixed charge and floating charge;**
2. **what happens when creditors have floating charges over the same assets; and**
3. **what if the Bank of Hastings' floating charge was not validly registered.**

Tunde is not a lawyer, so it is important that your explanation is clear and simple. He is intelligent and astute, and will insist on understanding everything, so you will need to provide brief legal explanations where appropriate.

Thanks

Partner

Note to candidates:

Please assume that all issues in relation to client care/money laundering have already been dealt with by the partner.

*   *   *

■ YOUR TURN

Have a go at answering question 2, remembering the guidance on pages 57–58.
- Refer to the structured approach in the SRA's assessment criteria on page 58.
- Create a list of the most salient points raised by the question.
- Timings are important: you will need to prepare and write your answer in 30 minutes.

SQE1 Functioning legal knowledge link
Remember from chapter 5 of *Revise SQE: Business Law and Practice* that it is possible for lenders to agree to a different arrangement as to their relative priority by entering into a deed of priority.

EVALUATING YOUR ANSWER

When you have attempted question 2, mark it yourself against the SQE2 legal writing assessment criteria. Do you think your attempt met the threshold standard?

Now compare your attempt with the following key legal points and two sample answers to question 2. A circled number indicates that commentary is provided for this part of the answer. The commentary will explain whether or not the sample is likely to meet the threshold SQE2 standard.

➡️Key legal points: Question 2

- Businesses may have loans from banks or other credit providers. These loans are often secured.
- A mortgage involves the transfer of legal title to the mortgagee (lender) with re-conveyance/transfer back to the mortgagor (borrower) when the debt is satisfied. It gives the lender an immediate right to possession, and in the case of land, a mortgage is usually created by a fixed charge by deed.
- A fixed charge is a charge taken over a particular asset or assets. The consent of the lender is required in order to deal with the assets.
- A floating charge is a charge taken over a particular class of asset(s) owned from time to time (eg tangible stock and/or intangible intellectual property) and can only be granted by a company/LLP. The company can deal with the asset(s) without the consent of the lender until crystallisation, as until then, it 'floats over' rather than 'fixes on' the assets.
- On crystallisation, a floating charge 'fixes' on the assets in the particular class at that time and it becomes a fixed charge. Crystallisation usually occurs when a company becomes insolvent or any other event occurs which the charge specifies will cause crystallisation (eg non-payment, ceasing to trade or other default).
- Fixed charges take priority over floating charges. Where there are multiple validly created charges of the same type, the first in time (based on the date of creation) will have priority unless the document creating the floating charge contains a negative pledge clause and the later fixed charge has notice of this prohibition at the time when it takes its charge.
- A charge that is not registered in time is void against a liquidator or any creditor of the company (ss 859H(3) and (4) Companies Act 2006). The debt will be payable immediately, but will be unsecured (s 859H(4)).

◼ SAMPLE ANSWER 1 TO QUESTION 2

[The law firm's address and contact details]

Poppy's Pots
The Haven
Swan Lane
Hastings TN34 9LT

1 June 202#

Dear Tunde

Poppy's Pots Ltd – Security of loans

It was a pleasure talking to you yesterday – I'm very pleased to hear of the growth of Poppy's Pots Ltd. ❶

As promised, I have set out below a brief summary of the different types of secured loans that Poppy's Pots might have, what happens when two banks have a floating charge over the same assets and what happens if charges are not validly registered. ❷

1.   Mortgage, fixed charge and floating charge

Lenders usually require security for a loan. This can be by way of a mortgage, a fixed charge or a floating charge. In the event of insolvency, lenders with secured loans have priority over those with unsecured loans. There is a particular order of priority for the recovery of secured loans that is prescribed by statute: loans secured by a mortgage get first priority, followed by fixed charge holders, and then floating charge holders (provided the charges are validly registered). ❸

Mortgage

Security that is subject to a legal mortgage is effectively held by the lender. The legal title is transferred to the lender in exchange for the loan. When the loan is repaid, the legal title is transferred back to the borrower. ❹

The Bank of Hastings has a legal mortgage over the garden office. So, the legal title to the garden office was transferred to the Bank in exchange for the loan. When Poppy's Pots repays the loan, the legal title of the office will be transferred back. If Poppy's Pots fails to pay the debt, the Bank of Hastings will have the immediate right to possess the garden office.

Fixed charge

A fixed charge is a charge taken over a particular asset. Poppy's Pots would retain the legal title to the assets, but the consent of the lender would be required to deal with the assets.

Jellogs Bank is offering to lend Poppy's Pots £740,000 subject to a fixed charge over the new office space and showroom. This means that Jellogs' consent would be needed to sell that office in the future.

Floating charge

A floating charge is a charge taken over a particular class of assets that usually changes from time to time, such as the stock. The borrower is allowed to deal with the assets, until and unless a specified trigger event occurs. ❺ Common trigger events include ceasing to trade or non-payment. If such a trigger event occurs, the charge then becomes fixed over the assets as they existed at the time of the event. The borrower is then unable to deal with those assets without the lender's consent. If the charge is over stock, which is vital for a trading company, this restriction can be extremely debilitating.

The Bank of Hastings currently has a floating charge over all Poppy's Pots' stock. So, the company can trade its pots without the Bank's consent until and unless a trigger event occurs. Obviously, if the company ever experiences any financial issues, I would strongly advise that you liaise with the Bank at the earliest opportunity. ❻

2. Floating charges over the same assets

Where there is more than one floating charge over the same asset, the first one created normally takes priority over later charges.

So, assuming the Bank of Hastings' floating charge over Poppy's Pots' stock (being the pots) was validly registered, that charge would take priority over any later floating charges created over Poppy's Pots' stock.

The Bank of Hastings would have the right to any proceeds from the sale of Poppy's Pots' stock to satisfy its outstanding debt, and if there was any stock still available to sell, Jellogs Bank could then receive the proceeds from the sale of those remaining pots.

3. What if the Bank of Hastings' floating charge was not validly registered?

If a charge is not validly registered, and the borrower then goes into insolvency, the loan would become immediately payable, but be void against a liquidator or a creditor of the company. The loan would be treated as an unsecured debt.

You said you recall the Bank of Hastings charge being registered. I will check the records at Companies House to confirm this position. If it is not validly registered, and Poppy's Pots takes a loan from Jellogs Bank giving Jellogs a floating charge over Poppy's Pots' stock, Jellogs' charge over the stock would take priority over any floating charge held by Bank of Hastings. **7**

If you would like to discuss the security of your loans further, do please contact me.

I wish you the best of luck with your search for the right premises.

Yours sincerely

Partner

COMMENTARY

1 Note that the letter refers to the company by its full name, and not the abbreviation used in the partner's instruction to the candidate. Generally, you should avoid defining terms in a letter to the client as this may have the effect of making the letter appear too 'legal', which may detract from the aim of the letter being client- and recipient-focused.

2 As with sample answer 1 to question 1, it is good practice to inform the client at the beginning of the letter about its purpose and what information they can glean from it. This ensures that the letter is client-focused.

3 This provides a bit of explanation to the client about the difference between secured and unsecured loans and the priority of secured loans. Without this background context, the client would not be able to clearly determine why there is such an importance between the different types of security. Again, this background enables the advice and the content of the letter to be clear and client-focused, using language which is appropriate to the recipient.

4 Note how the legal principle is stated, and then the law is applied to the client's situation. This demonstrates the advice being client- and recipient-focused, while applying the law correctly to the client's situation. This approach is adopted throughout the letter.

5 Note that the term 'crystallisation' is not used when explaining this point. This is an example of legal terminology that might be considered unnecessary. It is important to use clear, precise, concise and acceptable language which is appropriate to the recipient.

6 This last sentence is included just to advise the client of how important it is to liaise with the Bank if the financial position changes, while acknowledging that it is not currently relevant.

7 Clear explanation of the next steps is provided here, comprehensively demonstrating the candidate's application of the law to Poppy's Pots' situation.

Does this answer meet the threshold?

The sample answer above contains all of the information that the client requires and that the candidate has been asked to provide. It is therefore likely to meet the threshold standard for the SQE2 legal writing assessment. Clear, succinct and accurate language is used throughout, and the letter adopts a logical structure, using headings and sub-headings and numbering. It refers to the parties concerned by name (Poppy's Pots, or the various banks, rather than just 'the lender' or 'the borrower'), making the letter more recipient-focused. Remember to bear in mind the assessment criteria as you form your answer so that you address all of the SRA's requirements.

Now consider the second sample answer to question 2.

■ SAMPLE ANSWER 2 TO QUESTION 2

[The law firm's address and contact details]

Poppy's Pots
The Haven
Swan Lane
Hastings TN34 9LT

1 June 202#

Dear Poppy Pots **❶**

Secured loans

You asked me to write to you to follow up our recent phone conversation. **❷**

1.   Mortgage, fixed charge and floating charge

A mortgage is a secured loan. Normally the security is a property. For example, you might have a mortgage over your residential home. Mortgages are often executed as a deed, meaning that they are signed in the presence of witnesses. **❸** If you fail to pay your mortgage, the lender will have the right to repossess your house. **❹** This is often the key condition that is emphasised in any mortgage. **❺**

A fixed charge is when the security is over a permanent, unchanging asset, such as property or plant and machinery.

A floating charge is when the security is over an asset that might change from day to day, such as a company's stock. **❻**

2.   Floating charges over the same assets

It is possible to have charges over the same assets. For example, a property might be subject to a first and second charge. This means that if the borrower defaulted and the security was enforced, the first charge holder would have priority over the second charge holder. So the second charge holder would only be able to recover their debt after the first charge holder had been paid in full. **❼** A floating charge over property would not be appropriate as property as an asset doesn't generally change from day to day (unless a company was buying and selling property as part of its trade, in which case the property would effectively be treated as 'stock'). **❽** A floating charge could be given over a company's current bank account. If the borrower defaulted, this would normally be considered an event of crystallisation so the floating charge would crystallise and become a fixed charge over the company's current bank account as it was at the time of the event of crystallisation. **❾**

3. Invalid charge

Charges should be registered at Companies House by submitting Form MR01 ⑩ with a fee. The form should set out the details of the charge – the date it was created, the charge holder, etc. Details of any negative pledge clause should also be included in this form as it is a public document that is available by a simple search at Companies House. ⑪

If a charge is not validly registered at Companies House, it is void against a company, creditor, liquidator and administrator in accordance with section 859 Companies Act. ⑫ The charge is effectively treated as an unsecured charge. As you know, unsecured charge holders rank very low in the statutory priority of creditors and thus the loan is unlikely to be repaid in full in such an event. ⑬

If you need any further assistance, please do not hesitate to contact me – I should be happy to help. ⑭

Yours

Partner

COMMENTARY

① The letter should be addressed to Tunde Belucchi, as the managing director of Poppy's Pots, not to Poppy's Pots directly. Note also that the candidate has not stated the company's name correctly, which is Poppy's Pots.

② The opening sentence does not inform the client about the letter's purpose and what information they can glean from it.

③ This is irrelevant for the purposes of this letter. You must always be mindful of the instructions and be sure that the information contained in your letter addresses the problem(s) presented by the client.

④ This is incorrect. A legal mortgage transfers legal ownership of the mortgaged asset to the lender unless the asset is land. The instructions do not refer to Tunde's home being security for the business, so this is an example of failing to apply the law correctly to the client's situation.

⑤ This is irrelevant – see point 3 above.

⑥ There is no application of the law to the client's situation. How do mortgages and fixed and floating charges apply to the client? Why are they relevant to the client? The use of headings does help understanding, but the lack of context detracts from this. As with point 3 above, in the assessment you must address your client's situation in your letter; do not just state the law, but go on to explain how or why it relates to the client's issue(s). So here, the Bank of Hastings already has a floating charge over PPL's stock and Jellogs Bank wants a floating charge over the same asset. Jellogs Bank also wants a fixed charge over PPL's new office space.

⑦ The client was concerned with floating charges, not fixed charges. The advice provided is therefore not clear, nor client-focused. The law is not correctly applied to the client's situation, as the law applied relates to charge holders in general, not specifically to floating charge holders.

⑧ This does not explain the law with any clarity, nor does it relate back to the instructions. See point 3 above.

⑨ Crystallising events and 'crystallisation' are technical terms. The explanation of these terms in this letter is not client-focused. When writing a letter in the SQE2 assessment, be mindful of your reader and explain any law clearly and comprehensively.

(10) As with point 9 above, the reference to the form is too technical. It does not address the instructions and is not one of the three questions on which the candidate is asked to advise. Keep your reader in mind, and be sure to write clearly, concisely and comprehensively.

(11) Reference is made to a negative pledge clause without explanation as to what this is. The client may be unaware of its impact. In addition, consider whether this is relevant to what the client is asking.

(12) The client does not need to be advised of which section of the Companies Act addresses registration of charges. The client is not a lawyer and is unlikely to look this up. Remember to keep the letter client-focused.

(13) Again, there is no application of the law. The legal position of an unsecured creditor is stated, but not applied to the client's situation – if Bank of Hastings' floating charge was not validly registered, it would be treated as an unsecured creditor.

(14) 'I should be happy to help' is not an appropriate way to sign off a letter. It is too informal. Similarly, the candidate should have written 'Yours sincerely' rather than 'Yours' on the line below.

Does this answer meet the threshold?

When assessing the second letter against the SQE2 legal writing assessment criteria, it is unlikely that this letter would meet the threshold standard for the SQE2 legal writing assessment. Limited relevant facts are used, and the law is mostly correctly identified but not applied to the client's situation. The letter adopts a logical structure with headings and numbering correlating to the client's questions, which contributes to the clarity of the answer. However, more needs to be done to make the advice clear and recipient-focused. Remember the assessment criteria as you write your answer so that you address all of the SRA's requirements.

■ KEY POINT CHECKLIST

This chapter has covered the following key knowledge points:
- The SQE2 assessment criteria for legal writing and applying them in the context of business organisations, rules and procedures.
- A suggested structure for approaching an SQE2 legal writing question.
- Examples of answers in the format of letters, which are either likely or unlikely to meet the SQE2 threshold standard, with full commentary on their strengths and weaknesses.

■ SUMMARY AND REFLECTION

To meet the threshold standard in the SQE2 legal writing assessment, take your time to read the question properly, think about the legal points the question is asking of you and sketch out a short plan to follow for the structure of your letter.

Remember that the SQE2 assessment requires you to apply the law both correctly *and* comprehensively. You need to consider the relevant law and explain how it is applicable to the wider context of the client's scenario as well as to the more obvious narrow points.

You will be penalised in the assessment for using too much legal jargon or legalistic terms without explaining them properly, as the client recipient might not understand what you mean. Practise writing letters in client-friendly language that a non-lawyer reader would be able to understand.

Now take the time to reflect and consider what you might still need to work on, and whether you feel completely confident in your legal writing skills in the context of business organisations, rules and procedures.

4

Legal drafting

■ MAKE SURE YOU KNOW

This chapter deals with the skill of legal drafting in the context of business organisations, rules and procedures. Legal drafting in this area is one of the skills that will be assessed on day three of the SQE2 assessments (see the Introduction for more detail). Management decisions made by any business organisation should be documented. Businesses often obtain credit from banks that, together with applicable statute, can dictate how decisions are made and by whom. The procedural aspects of such decisions must be addressed correctly, precisely and concisely to promote clarity and understanding. It is therefore important that you read this revision guide once you are familiar with the contents of *Revise SQE: Business Law and Practice* and *Revise SQE: Contract Law*.

This chapter provides examples of how different scenarios relating to business organisations, rules and procedures, taxation for businesses, money laundering and financial services could arise in the context of a legal drafting SQE2 assessment.

■ SQE ASSESSMENT ADVICE

As you work through this chapter, remember to pay particular attention in your revision to:
- the methodical approach to the way in which the draft document is presented in the sample answers and how this could be applied generally
- the use of precise and concise language to ensure clarity and no ambiguity in the document
- the way in which the documents in the sample answers adapt precedents to develop a document that is logical, clear and correct
- how the documents in the sample answers identify the correct legal principles and address them correctly
- the way in which the sample answers are legally effective
- how the documents are sufficiently accurate in the context of the clients' situations and the relevant factual and legal issues
- the way in which ethical or professional conduct issues are identified and resolved in the sample answers.

See the Appendix for the SRA's performance indicators in legal drafting.

■ INTRODUCTION TO LEGAL DRAFTING IN BUSINESS ORGANISATIONS, RULES AND PROCEDURES

It is likely that your SQE2 assessment will replicate scenarios which occur in day-to-day legal practice. A key aspect of practising in the field of business organisations, rules and procedures is the ability to draft a legal document or parts of a legal document. Your SQE2 assessment in legal drafting will be based around reading a memo or email from a partner which asks you to draft a legal document or parts of a legal document for a client. You will be required to apply your knowledge of the legal areas raised by

the question to the specific scenario, and draft the relevant document or parts of the document for the client clearly and precisely. You may be asked to draft:
• from a precedent, or
• by amending a document already drafted, or
• without either of these documents.

This chapter will provide examples of how you can do this and meet the criteria for the SQE2 legal drafting assessment.

The key to success in your SQE2 legal drafting assessment is approaching the question in a methodical manner. Try adopting the following approach:
1. Once you have read the question, write down the key legal points addressing what the client is asking of you, including provisions that you feel need to be included in your document.
2. Identify where in the document these provisions should be inserted and/or how the drafting should be structured to create a logical layout of the legal provisions. Consider whether the drafting could be made clearer using paragraphs, headings and/or defined terms, being mindful of the need for the entire document to be consistent. Review any precedents to follow for the structure of your legal drafting.
3. Draft your document.
4. Review your answer making sure it addresses the question while keeping in mind the SQE2 legal drafting assessment criteria.

Assessment technique

When reviewing your answer, be aware of any defined terms and check that definitions are accurate and enable your document to be legally correct. Similarly, review the consistency of the numbered paragraphs in your document. Check that any drafting notes and square brackets have been deleted where appropriate.

SQE2 legal drafting assessment criteria

Try to remember these points as you construct your answer:

Skills
1. Use clear, precise, concise and acceptable language.
2. Structure the document appropriately and logically.

Application of law
3. Draft a document which is legally correct.
4. Draft a document which is legally comprehensive, identifying any ethical and professional conduct issues and exercising judgement to resolve them honestly and with integrity.

In chapter 3 of *Revise SQE: Business Law and Practice*, we considered limited companies and decision-making. Question 1 below demonstrates how your knowledge of this topic could be tested in the context and format of a SQE2 legal drafting assessment.

■ QUESTION 1

Email to candidate

From: Partner
Sent: 1 July 202#
To: Candidate
Subject: Changing The Petrollers Ltd to The Elecs Ltd

We have been advising The Petrollers Ltd for many years, since its incorporation in 2017. The company operates a car dealership, which used to focus mainly on the sale of petrol cars. The company has adopted the Model Articles without any amendments.

Preet Gupta is the Managing Director. She recently telephoned me saying that she and the Finance Director, Ali Mahmood, thought the name of the company ought to be changed, as they felt it portrayed the wrong image for the dealership. Both Preet and Ali would like the name to be changed to 'The Elecs Ltd' as soon as possible.

Fuad Iqbal is the company secretary and chairs the company's general meetings. All three officers have 100 shares each. There are no other shareholders. The company number is X3929009.

The Petrollers Ltd's office address (which is the same as its registered office) is Wilborne House, 10 Wilborne Road, London W3 2BD. Preet, Ali and Fuad have a strategy meeting tomorrow 9 AM–5 PM and Preet wondered if the name change could be addressed at 8.30 AM tomorrow morning, before the strategy meeting which she will be chairing. The company always deals with company matters by way of meetings.

I have attached the firm's template pack for Company Meeting Minutes comprising of a draft:

a) **notice of a general meeting (Attachment 1); and**
b) **format for the minutes of a general meeting (Attachment 2).**

Could you please amend the notice and minutes as you think appropriate to address the proposed change of name?

Thanks

Partner

Attachment 1

Template notice of general meeting

Company number [   ]

NOTICE OF GENERAL MEETING

NOTICE is given that a general meeting of the company will be held on [*insert date*] at [*insert time*] at [*insert address*], for the following purposes:

ORDINARY RESOLUTION[S]

To consider and, if thought fit, approve the following resolution[s] that will be proposed as [an] ordinary resolution[s]:

[*insert text of proposed ordinary resolutions*]

SPECIAL RESOLUTION[S]

To consider and, if thought fit, approve the following resolution[s] that will be proposed as [a] special resolution[s]:

[*insert text of proposed special resolutions*]

By order of the board

....

[*insert name of company secretary or director*]

Registered Office: [*insert registered office address*]
[*insert date*]

PROXY NOTICE

A member of the Company entitled to attend and vote at the meeting is entitled to appoint a proxy to attend and vote in his place. A proxy may demand, or join in demanding a poll. A proxy need not be a member of the Company.

[CONSENT TO SHORT NOTICE [if applicable]

We, the undersigned, being [all the members] having OR a majority in number of the members [having, and together holding not less than [90 OR 95 OR [*insert other figure*]]% in nominal value of the shares giving] the right to attend and vote at the general meeting of the company to be held at [*insert time*] on [*insert date*] at [*insert place*] consent to the meeting being called on shorter notice than that specified in the Companies Act 2006 or in the Company's articles of association has been given.]

Dated:

Name of shareholder:

Attachment 2

Template general meeting minutes

Minutes of a general meeting
Company number [NUMBER]
[NAME OF COMPANY]

Minutes of a meeting of [   ] (the 'Company')
Held at:
On:
Present:
In attendance:

1. Notice and quorum

1.1 It was reported that due notice of the meeting was given to the shareholders of the Company in accordance with the Companies Act 2006 and the Company's articles of association.
1.2 The Chair noted that a quorum was present at the meeting. Accordingly, the Chair declared the meeting open.

2. Business of the meeting

The Chair reported that the meeting had been called to [*insert details of what is to be addressed in the meeting*].

3. Resolutions

3.1 The Chair declared that the shareholders' approval was required to: [*insert details*].
3.2 The Chair proposed the following resolution to be passed as an [*ordinary/ special resolution*]:
Ordinary resolution

Special resolution

3.3 The Chair noted that the resolution(s) set out in paragraph 3.2 were passed by a [% of votes] as an [ordinary/special] resolution.

4. Close

There being no further business the Chair declared the General Meeting closed.

....

Signed by   Date

*   *   *

■ YOUR TURN

Have a go at answering question 1, remembering the guidance on pages 73–74.
- Refer to the structured approach in the SRA's assessment criteria on page 74.
- Create a list of the most salient legal points raised by the question and the requirements for the relevant drafting to implement the client's instructions.
- Timings are important: you will need to prepare and write your answer in 45 minutes.

SQE1 Functioning legal knowledge link

Remember from chapter 3 of *Revise SQE: Business Law and Practice* that some company decisions require the shareholders' approval by an ordinary resolution (OR) or special resolution (SR), as set out in the Companies Act 2006 and the company's articles. In addition, company decision-making involves a number of reporting requirements and formalities.

EVALUATING YOUR ANSWER

When you have attempted question 1, mark it yourself against the SQE2 legal drafting assessment criteria. Do you think your attempt met the threshold standard?

Now compare your attempt with the following key legal points and two sample answers to question 1. A circled number beside the text indicates that commentary is provided for this part of the answer. The commentary will explain whether or not the sample is likely to meet the threshold SQE2 standard.

➡️Key legal points: Question 1

Note, references to CA 2006 are references to the Companies Act 2006.

- An SR is required for a company to change its name (s 77(1) CA 2006).
- A BM1-GM-BM2 format would be appropriate to action a change of name where decisions are carried out in meetings, or an alternative could be substituting written resolutions for meetings (remember the abbreviations used in *Revise SQE: Business Law and Practice*: BM for board meeting and GM for general meeting). BM1 would arrange for the calling of the GM; GM would address the OR and/or SR put to the members, while BM2 would address any filings or follow-up action arising from the GM.
- At least 14 clear days' notice of a GM must be given to shareholders, although this can be shortened by agreement of the members. The majority (in number) of shareholders, who collectively hold 90% or more of the voting rights (subject to the articles specifying a higher percentage, up to a maximum of 95% (s 307 CA 2006)) must agree to the short notice for it to be effective.
- Section 311 requires that any notice of GM must contain the date, time and place of the meeting, the full text of any SR proposed and sufficient detail of any ORs (s 283 CA 2006) and a proxy notice.
- After the shareholders have approved the change of name, Form NM01 and a copy of the SR passed by the shareholders approving the name change must be filed at Companies House.
- A change of name takes effect immediately.
- Minutes of GMs must be available for inspection by the members at the registered office (ss 355, 358 CA 2006).

■ SAMPLE ANSWER 1 TO QUESTION 1

Company number X3929009

NOTICE OF GENERAL MEETING

THE PETROLLERS LTD (the 'Company')

NOTICE is given that a general meeting of the Company will be held on 2 July 202# at 8.30 AM at Wilborne House, 10 Wilborne Road, London W3 2BD, for the following purpose: ❶

SPECIAL RESOLUTION

To consider and, if thought fit, approve the following resolution that will be proposed as a special resolution:

That the name of the Company be changed from The Petrollers Ltd to The Elecs Ltd ❷

By order of the board

....

Fuad Iqbal

Company Secretary
Registered Office: Wilborne House, 10 Wilborne Road, London W3 2BD
2 July 202# ❸

PROXY NOTICE

A member of the Company entitled to attend and vote at the meeting is entitled to appoint a proxy to attend and vote in his place. A proxy may demand, or join in demanding a poll. A proxy need not be a member of the Company.

CONSENT TO SHORT NOTICE

We, the undersigned, being all the members holding 100% in nominal value of the shares giving the right to attend and vote at the general meeting of the company to be held at 8.30 AM on 2 July 202# at Wilborne House, 10 Wilborne Road, London W3 2BD consent to the meeting being called on shorter notice than that specified in the Companies Act 2006 or in the Company's articles of association has been given. ❹

Dated:

Signed by

Preet Gupta:

Ali Mahmood:

Fuad Iqbal: ❺

Minutes of a general meeting
Company number X3929009
THE PETROLLERS LTD

Minutes of a meeting of The Petrollers Ltd (the 'Company') ⑥

Held at: Wilborne House, 10 Wilborne Road, London W3 2BD
On: 2 July 202#
Present: Fuad Iqbal (Chair), Preet Gupta and Ali Mahmood
In attendance: ⑦

1. Notice and quorum

1.1 It was reported that due notice of the meeting was given to the shareholders of the Company in accordance with the Companies Act 2006 and the Company's articles of association.
1.2 The Chair noted that a quorum was present at the general meeting. Accordingly, the Chair declared the meeting open. ⑧

2. Business of the meeting

The Chair reported that the general meeting had been convened to change the name of the Company from The Petrollers Ltd to The Elecs Ltd. ⑨

3. Resolution

3.1 The Chair declared that the shareholders' approval was required to change the name of the Company from The Petrollers Ltd to The Elecs Ltd.
3.2 The Chair proposed that the following resolution be passed as a special resolution. ⑩
Special resolution
'That the company name be changed from The Petrollers Ltd to The Elecs Ltd'
3.3 The Chair noted that the resolution set out in paragraph 3.2 was passed by 100% of votes as a special resolution. ⑪

4. Close

There being no further business the Chair declared the meeting closed.

....

Signed by Fuad Iqbal   Date ⑫

COMMENTARY

(Points 1–5 relate to the notice; points 6 onwards relate to the minutes.)

1. The instructions provided information on the company name, number, address and details of the date, time and place of the meeting. All of this information must be entered in the appropriate place to ensure the document is appropriately and logically structured and legally correct.

2. The template has been amended to reflect that there is only one resolution being proposed, ensuring clarity and accuracy. Note how the full text of the SR to be proposed in the GM is set out, including what the name is to be changed from and to. Clear, precise and accurate language is used, ensuring the wording is legally correct.

3. Amendments have been made to the template to ensure that the structure of the document is appropriate and logical, and the notice and minutes are legally correct; for example, the date of the notice and the meeting and the registered office were added to the draft and the square brackets removed to create a correct and precise draft.

4. Note the insertion of the wording as set out by statute, to address shareholders' rights to consent to short notice, which must be included if the notice period is reduced. The draft reflects the members' shareholding clearly and accurately. This is an example of amending a draft to ensure the document is legally correct.

5. The names of the shareholders who need to sign the consent to short notice have been inserted to ensure the document is accurate. Doing this also supports the logical structure of the draft.

6. Note how The Petrollers is defined as the 'Company' from the beginning of the Notice and the Minutes when The Petrollers is first mentioned, demonstrating a logical structure which assists the clarity and precision of the document.

7. Information about who is present, in attendance and chairing the meeting was given in the instructions. Note how this information is inputted in the appropriate places here, enabling the document to be legally correct. If applicable, the names and capacity of any observers/advisers attending the meeting would be included under 'In attendance', e.g. 'A. N. Other (solicitor)'.

8. All minutes should have a paragraph addressing the quorum and the notice having validly been given, as without these the meeting might not be validly held. The paragraph is legally correct and factually accurate.

9. Note how the details of what is to be addressed in the meeting are set out clearly and precisely.

10. There is only one resolution to pass here – to change the name of the company. It is important to use clear, precise, concise and acceptable language, ensuring the document is comprehensive.

11. The type of resolution to be passed must be specified. We are informed in the instructions that there are three shareholders who are directors/officers of the company. All will be attending at the meeting and all hold 100 shares each. All three shareholders will need to approve the resolution to change the name of the company for it to be passed, so 100% of the votes would need to be in favour of the change. This is an example of drafting a document which is precise and legally correct.

12. It is important that the minutes are signed by the chair so they can be used as evidence if required (s 355 CA).

Does this answer meet the threshold?

The sample answer above contains all the information to enable the client to complete this change of business name from a legal standpoint. It follows a logical structure, uses clear and precise language and is legally correct. It is therefore likely to meet the threshold standard for the SQE2 legal drafting assessment. Note how each of the assessment criteria for legal drafting are dealt with.

Now consider the second sample answer to question 1.

■ SAMPLE ANSWER 2 TO QUESTION 1

Company number X3929009

NOTICE OF GENERAL MEETING

NOTICE is given that a general meeting of the company will be held on [3 July 202#] at 8.30 AM at Wilbourne House, 10 Wilbourne Road, London W3 2BD for the following purposes: ①

ORDINARY RESOLUTION ②

To consider and, if thought fit, approve the following resolution that will be proposed as an ordinary resolution:

That the name of the company be changed to The Elecs Ltd

By order of the board

....

Fuad Iqbal

Secretary
Registered Office: Wilbourne House, 10 Wilbourne Road, London W3 2BD
[insert date] ③

PROXY NOTICE

A member of the Company entitled to attend and vote at the meeting is entitled to appoint a proxy to attend and vote in his place. A proxy may demand, or join in demanding, a poll. A proxy need not be a member of the Company.

CONSENT TO SHORT NOTICE

We, the undersigned, being all the members having and together holding not less than 90% in nominal value of the shares giving the right to attend and vote at the general meeting of the company to be held at 8.30 AM on 3 July 202# at Wilbourne House, 10 Wilbourne Road, London W3 2BD consent to the meeting being called on shorter notice than that specified in the Companies Act 2006 or in the Company's articles of association has been given. ④

Dated:

Name of shareholder: ⑤

Minutes of a general meeting
Company number X3929001 ⑥
The Petrollers Ltd ('Company')

Minutes of a meeting of The Petrollers Ltd (the 'Company') ⑦

Held at: Wilbourne House, 10 Wilbourne Road, London W3 2BD
On: [insert date] ⑧
Present: Preet Gupta, Ali Mahmood, Fuad Iqbal ⑨
In attendance:

1. Notice and quorum

1.1 It was reported that due notice of the meeting was given to the shareholders of the Company in accordance with the Companies Act 2006 and the Company's articles of association.
1.2 The Chair further noted that a quorum was present at the meeting. Accordingly, the Chair declared the meeting open.

2. Business of the meeting

The Chair reported that the meeting had been called to pass the resolution set out in the notice of the meeting (the 'Resolution'). ⑩

3. Resolution

3.1 The Chair declared that the shareholders' approval was required to pass the resolution which would take place on a show of hands OR poll. ⑪
3.2 The Chair proposed the following resolution be passed as an ordinary resolution: ⑫

Ordinary resolution
That the Company's name be changed to The Elecs Ltd. ⑬
3.3 The Chair noted that the resolution set out in paragraph 3.2 was passed by 50% of votes as an ordinary resolution of the Company. ⑭

4. Close

There being no further business the Chair declared the meeting closed. ⑮

COMMENTARY

(Points 1–5 relate to the notice; points 6 onwards relate to the minutes.)

❶ The square bracket in precedent documents that are amended should be removed to ensure that the document is clear, precise and accurate and structured appropriately and logically. Note also that the candidate has included the wrong date, and has misspelt 'Wilborne' throughout their answer. This document is therefore not legally correct.
❷ This is not legally correct: to change a company's name, an SR is required.
❸ The date of the notice was provided in the instructions and should be inputted to ensure the document is legally correct and structured appropriately.
❹ Note the insertion of the wording as set out by statute, to address shareholders' rights to consent to short notice, which must be included if the notice period is

reduced. This is an example of amending a draft to ensure the document is legally correct.

5 Note the shareholders' names should be written into this document, as all three will be present and required to sign the notice in advance of the meeting. This enables the draft to be legally correct, appropriately structured and precise.

6 The company number is incorrect, resulting in a document that is not precise nor accurate.

7 The 'Company' is defined twice in the minutes and not at all in the notice. This is not correct and creates ambiguity. It is important when drafting to use clear, precise language and ensure the structure is appropriate and logical.

8 The date of the notice, consent to short notice and minutes should have been as directed in the instructing email. No date is inserted in the minutes, resulting in the document being inaccurate and imprecise.

9 The minutes do not identify who the chair is. This results in a document that is not precise, with the identity of the chair as referred to in later paragraphs not being clear.

10 Note how the template has been amended to reflect that only one resolution is proposed and passed at this meeting, to enable the minutes to be clear and precise. Precedents often contain square brackets and these should be deleted when they are not required or the drafting notes which they contain have been addressed, to ensure that the document is structured correctly and is clear, precise and legally correct. If documents are referred to in the minutes, they should be defined to ensure clarity.

11 The minutes must reflect what happened in the meeting. The reference to a poll vote would not be appropriate at this meeting as the candidate is instructed that all shareholders have an equal shareholding and will be attending the meeting. For the resolution to pass, all three shareholders must agree to the proposal. 'OR poll' should be deleted to ensure that the draft is clear and precise, and legally correct.

12 An SR, not OR, is required to change the name of a company. By not correcting this, the document is inaccurate and legally incorrect.

13 It would be good practice to refer to what the name should be changed from and to, to make the minutes more comprehensive.

14 This is not legally correct. The resolution would need to be approved by all three shareholders. See point 11 above.

15 Minutes should be signed and dated by the chair so that they may be used as evidence, therefore a space should be left for the signature and date.

Does this answer meet the threshold?

When assessing the second letter against the SQE2 legal drafting assessment criteria, it is unlikely that this letter would meet the threshold standard for the SQE2 legal drafting assessment. The language adopted is not always clear and precise, the document is poorly structured and the draft is not legally correct.

As you know, SQE2 can assess any of the areas on the SQE1 Business Law and Practice specification. Below is another example of how a different part of the specification could arise in the context of legal drafting on SQE2.

■ QUESTION 2

Email to candidate

From: Partner
Sent: 1 August 202#
To: Candidate
Subject: Acquisition of lease of Unit 5 The Onyx, Church Street, London N2 3PX

I met Isaac Lewis yesterday who is the Managing Director of Crumble Ltd, a company that bakes cakes and pastries for sandwich shops and cafes in Central London. The company was incorporated in 2018.

The company has until now been operating from a kitchen site in Watford. However, as the company is expanding and has more customers in the North London area, the directors feel it needs a site that is closer to its customers. Felix Lang, one of the three directors of Crumble owns Unit 5, The Onyx, Church Street, London N2 3PX (the 'Unit') which he thinks might be suitable for Crumble's purposes. Isaac visited the Unit with Sonia Bates, Crumble's third director, and all three directors agree that the Unit would satisfy Crumble's needs for a new, more central site.

Felix has agreed to grant Crumble a lease of the Unit for a trial one-year term commencing on 1 May 202# at a cost of £110,000 per annum. Crumble will have the option to renew the lease on the same terms, after the expiry of the first nine months. The other directors believe this to be a reasonable offer.

Isaac also wants to implement a change to Crumble's articles, to permanently disapply the application of Model Article 14, which the other directors think is sensible given the size of the company.

Crumble's directors are meeting later today at Crumble's registered office of 8 The Meadows, Finchley N22 3TL. Isaac would like to proceed with both the lease and the amendment to the articles as soon as possible. He would like to approve at today's board meeting a written resolution to be sent out to the shareholders in relation to the two matters, and send the resolution out today. Shareholders should return their signed resolutions for Sonia Bates' attention by hand or post to the company's registered office, or by email to sonia.bates@crumbles.com.

I attach a written resolution template which I found on file (Attachment 1). Please would you review and amend it to deal with the above issues so that it can be sent to the shareholders today. The company's current articles are also attached for your reference (Attachment 2); please amend as you see fit.

Thanks

Partner

Attachment 1

Template written resolution

Company number [   ]

COMPANIES ACT 2006
PRIVATE COMPANY LIMITED BY SHARES
WRITTEN RESOLUTION OF
[   ] Limited (the 'Company')
Circulated on:

Pursuant to Chapter 2 of Part 13 of the Companies 2006, the directors of the Company propose that the resolution[s] below be passed as [ordinary/special] resolution[s]:

Ordinary resolution[s]

Resolution[s]	For	Against
[text of resolution[s]]		

Special resolution[s]

Resolution[s]	For	Against
[text of resolution[s]]		

[If articles amended, a copy of the proposed revisions must accompany the written resolution.]

Please read the Explanatory Notes at the end of this document before you sign to agree to the resolution[s].

I am a person entitled to vote on the resolution[s] set out above on the circulation date and irrevocably agree to the resolution[s].

Signed ....

Date ....

Explanatory Notes
1. If you wish to vote in favour of a resolution, please put an 'X' in the 'For' box next to that resolution. If you wish to vote against a resolution, please put an 'X' in the 'Against' box next to that resolution, or leave both boxes next to that resolution blank.
2. Once you have signified your agreement to a resolution[s], you may not revoke your agreement.
3. If you agree to a resolution[s], please ensure that you sign and return this written resolution by [date]. If there are no resolutions you agree with, you do not need to do anything. You will not be deemed to agree if you fail to reply. If sufficient agreement has not been received for the resolution[s] by this date, the resolution[s] will lapse.

Attachment 2

Company number: X473321

COMPANIES ACT 2006
Private company limited by shares
ARTICLES OF ASSOCIATION
of
Crumble Ltd

1. The name of the company is Crumble Ltd.
2. The registered office of the company is to be situated in England and Wales.
3. The liability of the members is limited to the amount (if any) unpaid on the shares held by them.
4. The regulations constituting the Model Articles for a Private Company Limited by Shares in The Companies (Model Articles) Regulations 2008 ('Model Articles') shall apply to the company, subject to such exclusions and variations as may be set out below or effected hereafter from time to time in accordance with the provisions of the Companies Act 2006 and such Model Articles.

Dated 2 September 2018

*   *   *

■ YOUR TURN

Have a go at answering question 2, remembering the guidance on pages 73–74.
*   Refer to the structured approach in the SRA's assessment criteria on page 74.
*   Create a list of the most salient legal points raised by the question.
*   Timings are important: you will need to prepare and write your answer in 45 minutes.

SQE1 Functioning legal knowledge link
Remember from chapter 4 of *Revise SQE: Business Law and Practice* that directors' powers are set out in the company's articles. Directors may approve most property transactions involving the company under the general management powers (MA3). Substantial property transactions (SPTs) that fall within s 190 CA require shareholders' approval by way of an OR. To be an SPT, the transaction must be between the company and a director (not someone who is just a shareholder) or a connected person. If there is a breach of s 190 CA, the transaction is voidable (s 195 CA).

EVALUATING YOUR ANSWER

When you have attempted question 2, mark it yourself against the SQE2 legal drafting assessment criteria. Do you think your attempt met the threshold standard?

Now compare your attempt with the following key legal points and two sample answers to question 2. A circled number beside the text indicates that commentary is provided for this part of the answer. The commentary will explain whether or not the sample answer is likely to meet the threshold SQE2 standard.

> **➡Key legal points: Question 2**
>
> Note, references to CA 2006 are references to the Companies Act 2006.
>
> ---
>
> - SPTs that fall within s 190 CA 2006 require shareholders' approval by way of an OR.
> - An SPT involves the *acquisition/disposal* of a *non cash asset* where
>   - the parties involved are the company and a director or a person connected to a director; and
>   - the asset is substantial, ie its value is not £5k or less and is either more than £100k or more than 10% of the company's net asset value.
> - The shareholders of a private company limited by shares can pass resolutions either at a GM or as written resolutions (s 288 CA 2006).
> - Written resolutions must:
>   - be sent to all eligible members
>   - set out the wording of the resolution to which the shareholders' agreement is sought
>   - provide a statement setting out how a shareholder can signify their agreement to the resolution and the date by which this must be received, after which the resolution will lapse (s 291 CA 2006). If no date is provided, the resolution will lapse at the end of the period of 28 days beginning with the circulation date, unless the articles provide otherwise.
> - The articles of a company can be amended by SR (s 21 CA 2006). Shareholders must be provided with a draft of the proposed new articles either at the GM at which the change is proposed or with the written resolution. If passed, the new articles and a copy of the SR must be sent to the Registrar of Companies not later than 15 days after the resolution is passed (s 26(1) CA 2006). The new articles take effect when the resolution is passed.

■ SAMPLE ANSWER 1 TO QUESTION 2

Company number X473321

COMPANIES ACT 2006
PRIVATE COMPANY LIMITED BY SHARES
WRITTEN RESOLUTION OF
Crumble Ltd (the 'Company') ❶
Circulated on: 3 August 202#

Pursuant to Chapter 2 of Part 13 of the Companies 2006, the directors of the Company propose that the resolutions below be passed as ordinary and special resolutions:

Ordinary resolution: ❷

Resolution[s]	For	Against
That the Company enter into a lease of Unit 5, The Onyx, Church Street, London N2 3PV with Felix Lang, a director of the Company, for one year commencing on 1 May 202# for £110,000 per annum, with the option to renew the lease on the same terms after the expiry of the first nine months.		

Special resolution: ❸

Resolution[s]	For	Against
That the draft articles of association attached be adopted as the articles of association of the Company in substitution for, and to the exclusion of, the existing articles of association.		

Please read the Explanatory Notes at the end of this document before you sign to agree to the resolutions. ❹

I am a person entitled to vote on the resolution set out above on the circulation date and irrevocably agree to the resolution.

Signed ....

Date ....

Explanatory Notes

1. If you wish to vote in favour of a resolution, please put an 'X' in the 'For' box next to that resolution. If you wish to vote against a resolution, please put an 'X' in the 'Against' box next to that resolution or leave both boxes next to that resolution blank.
2. Once you have signified your agreement to a resolution, you may not revoke your agreement.
3. If you agree to a resolution[s], please ensure that you record your vote as instructed in 1 above, and sign and date this document where indicated above and return it to the Company by hand or by post to Crumble Ltd, 8 The Meadows, Finchley N22 3TL, or by email to sonia.bates@crumbles.com by 29 August 202#. ❺ If there are no resolutions you agree with, you do not need to do anything. You will not be deemed to agree if you fail to reply. If sufficient agreement has not been received for the resolution[s] by this date, the resolution[s] will lapse. ❻

Company number: X473321

COMPANIES ACT 2006
Private company limited by shares
Draft ARTICLES OF ASSOCIATION
of
Crumble Ltd

1. The name of the company is Crumble Ltd.
2. The registered office of the company is to be situated in England and Wales.
3. The liability of the members is limited to the amount (if any) unpaid on the shares held by them.
4. The regulations constituting the Model Articles for a Private Company Limited by Shares in The Companies (Model Articles) Regulations 2008 ('Model Articles') shall apply to the company, subject to such exclusions and variations as may be set out below or effected hereafter from time to time in accordance with the provisions of the Companies Act 2006 and such Model Articles.
5. Model Article 14 shall not apply to the company. ❼

COMMENTARY

(Points 1–6 refer to the written resolutions; point 7 refers to the articles of association.)

1 Note how the Company is defined at the beginning of the resolution and then the defined term is used throughout the document, ensuring clarity and precision.

2 Note the amendments to reflect there is one OR and one SR proposed. The amendments have been made using clear, precise and acceptable language in a logical place in the document.

3 The details of the OR and SR have been set out clearly, precisely and accurately. The OR expressly states that the lease is to be acquired from Felix Lang, a director, while the SR expressly refers to the draft revised articles attached to the written resolution.

4 This sentence provides a link to the Explanatory Notes, providing a logical structure to the document. To be legally correct, the Explanatory Notes must accompany the written resolution,

5 Details of how the document should be returned to the Company were missing in the template. This information has been added, providing details of both the address for hand or postal delivery and an email address for delivery by email to ensure the document is clear, precise and legally correct.

6 A lapse date should be specified in the written resolution, and this has been provided clearly, precisely and accurately, providing legally correct information in a logical position in the document.

7 Note the insertion of a new paragraph 5 to reflect the amendment and removal of Model Article 14. The most appropriate place for this amendment is the creation of a new paragraph, and by inserting this new paragraph 5, the revised articles set out the comprehensive articles that are legally correct, if the written resolution is passed. The candidate has correctly not included a date, as the revised articles would only be effective when approved by the shareholders.

Does this answer meet the threshold?

The sample answer above contains all of the information that the client required to implement the client's instructions. It is therefore likely to meet the threshold standard for the SQE2 legal drafting assessment. The language adopted is clear and precise, it is well structured with headings and numbering where appropriate and is legally correct and comprehensive.

Now consider the second sample answer to question 2.

SAMPLE ANSWER 2 TO QUESTION 2

Company number X473321

COMPANIES ACT 2006
PRIVATE COMPANY LIMITED BY SHARES
WRITTEN RESOLUTION OF
Crumble Ltd (the 'Company') **1**
Circulated on: **2**

Pursuant to Chapter 2 of Part 13 of the Companies 2006, the directors of the Company propose that the resolutions below be passed:

Ordinary resolution[s]

Resolution[s]	For	Against
To permit the company to lease premises from Felix Lang. **3**		

Special resolution[s]

Resolution[s]	For	Against
To disapply model article 14. Save for this amendment, all other articles set out in the Company's articles shall continue to apply. **4**		

Please read the explanatory notes **5** at the end of this document before you sign to agree to the resolutions.

I am a person entitled to vote on the resolution set out above on the circulation date and irrevocably agree to the resolution.

Signed ....

Date ....

Explanatory Notes

1. If you wish to vote in favour of a resolution, please put an 'X' in the 'For' box next to that resolution. If you wish to vote against a resolution, please put an 'X' in the 'Against' box next to that resolution or leave both boxes next to that resolution blank.
2. Once you have signified your agreement to a resolution, you may not revoke your agreement.
3. If you agree to a resolution[s], please ensure that you record your vote as instructed in 1 above, and sign and date this document where indicated above and return it to the Company by hand or by post or by email **6** by [date]. **7** If there are no resolutions you agree with, you do not need to do anything. You will not be deemed to agree if you fail to reply. If sufficient agreement has not been received for the resolution[s] by this date, the resolution[s] will lapse.

Company number: X473321

COMPANIES ACT 2006
Private company limited by shares
ARTICLES OF ASSOCIATION
of
Crumble Ltd

1. The name of the company is Crumble Ltd.
2. The registered office of the company is to be situated in England and Wales.
3. The liability of the members is limited to the amount (if any) unpaid on the shares held by them.
4. The regulations constituting the Model Articles for a Private Company Limited by Shares in The Companies (Model Articles) Regulations 2008 ('Model Articles') shall apply to the company, subject to such exclusions and variations as may be set out below or effected hereafter from time to time in accordance with the provisions of the Companies Act 2006 and such Model Articles. ❽

Dated 2 September 2018

COMMENTARY

(Points 1–7 refer to the written resolutions; point 8 refers to the articles of association.)

❶ As with sample answer 1 to question 2, Company is defined in this document and the term is consistently applied to mean 'Crumble Ltd'.

❷ There is no circulation date specified. This creates uncertainty in relation to the lapse date.

❸ The details of the lease between the Company and Felix Lang are not clear or precise. There is scope for ambiguity and/or uncertainty.

❹ The revisions to the Company's articles are set out, but the revised articles that are attached to the written resolution should be referenced. The revised articles will also need to be sent to the Registrar of Companies when the resolution is passed. See point 8 below however; the candidate has failed to revise the articles.

❺ Explanatory notes are referred to in lower case here, but then later in the resolution, this term is capitalised. Again, this creates ambiguity and/or uncertainty and demonstrates a lack of precision.

❻ No address is provided for post, hand or email delivery. The document should be legally comprehensive and precise, so this fails to meet the assessment criteria.

❼ A lapse date for the resolution should be provided for clarity and precision.

❽ No revised wording to the articles is provided. The written resolution fails to be comprehensive or provide a document which is legally correct for the client's purposes.

Does this answer meet the threshold?

When assessing the second draft against the SQE2 legal drafting assessment criteria, it is unlikely that this letter would meet the threshold standard for the SQE2 legal drafting assessment. The language used is not always clear and precise, information is omitted thereby creating ambiguity and/or uncertainty, and the document is not legally correct or comprehensive.

■ KEY POINT CHECKLIST

This chapter has covered the following key knowledge points:
- The SQE2 assessment criteria for legal drafting and applying them in the context of business organisations, rules and procedures.
- A suggested structure for approaching an SQE2 legal drafting question.
- Examples of drafts which are either likely or unlikely to meet the threshold standard, with full commentary on their strengths and weaknesses.

■ SUMMARY AND REFLECTION

When tackling an SQE2 legal drafting assessment, you need to take your time to read the instructions properly, think about the legal points affecting what the client is asking of you, and consider any precedents to follow for the structure of your draft.

Remember that you are being assessed on whether you draft a document/part of a document which addresses the law correctly *and* comprehensively. You will need to consider the relevant law and draft a document which is legally correct in the context of the client's scenario to avoid being penalised in the assessment.

To support your revision, practise drafting documents using clear, precise, concise and acceptable language; any ambiguity will mean that your draft is not accurate and you will lose marks in the assessment.

Now take the time to reflect and consider what aspect of this written skill you might still need to work on, and whether you feel completely confident in your legal drafting skills in the context of business organisations, rules and procedures.

Final words

We hope that the guidance and examples contained in this book have helped to put into context how to use your practice skills to ensure you reach the SQE2 grading criteria. Remember, above all, this is an assessment and the examiner needs to see evidence that you have met the criteria in order for you to pass the threshold. Always keep this in the back of your mind when taking your SQE2 assessments.

While this book is designed to aid your learning and provide helpful tips on how to pass your SQE2 assessments, it is no substitute for practice. All skills are improved with repetition and refining your technique, and legal skills are no exception to this rule. Take any opportunity you can to write letters, draft legal documents and practise your interviewing and advocacy skills. Reflect carefully on your performance after each exercise:
- What could you have done better?
- Did you meet all of the grading criteria applicable to that particular skill?
- Do you need to fill any gaps in your legal knowledge?

Constant practice and self-reflection are the keys to success.

Finally, the team at *Revise SQE* wish you the best of luck in your SQE2 assessments!

Appendix

PERFORMANCE INDICATORS FOR SQE2
CASE AND MATTER ANALYSIS ASSESSMENT CRITERIA

Skills	Indicators demonstrating competence	Indicators that do not demonstrate competence
Identify relevant facts	• The candidate selects facts that are important in ensuring the client's needs/objectives are met, or are relevant to the legal analysis, from the documentation provided	• The candidate refers to all facts from the documentation, regardless of whether or not they are important in meeting the client's objectives or relevant to their legal analysis • The candidate refers only to irrelevant facts • The candidate does not refer to sufficient relevant facts to support the legal analysis
Provide client-focused advice (ie advice that demonstrates an understanding of the problem from the client's point of view and what the client wants to achieve, not just from a legal perspective)	• The candidate demonstrates an understanding of the client's problem from the client's perspective • The candidate addresses the client's legal problem, any relevant commercial considerations and/or the client's personal circumstances, priorities, objectives and constraints	• The candidate does not approach or appreciate the client's problem from the client's perspective • The candidate does not focus on the issues identified by the client
Use clear, precise, concise and acceptable language	• The reader understands the candidate's use of language and clarity of expression • The candidate avoids unnecessary technical terms/legal jargon	• The reader struggles to understand the candidate's use of language; the answer lacks clarity and/or is poorly expressed • The reader's understanding is adversely affected by the density, length or brevity of the answer • The candidate uses unnecessary technical terms/legal jargon

Law	Indicators demonstrating competence	Indicators that do not demonstrate competence
Apply the law correctly to the client's situation	• The candidate identifies the relevant fundamental legal principles in accordance with the SQE2 assessment specification and applies them correctly to the facts of the client's case	• The candidate does not identify and correctly apply the relevant legal principles to the facts of the client's case • The candidate does not apply the relevant legal principles in a way that addresses the client's needs and concerns
Apply the law comprehensively to the client's situation, identifying any ethical and professional conduct issues and exercising judgement to resolve them honestly and with integrity	• The candidate's legal analysis is sufficiently detailed in the context of the client's case, eg assessing information to identify key issues and risks; reaching reasonable conclusions supported by relevant evidence • Where relevant, the candidate recognises ethical issues and exercises effective judgement in addressing them in accordance with the SRA Principles and rules of professional conduct	• The candidate's legal analysis is not sufficiently detailed in the context of the client's case, eg the candidate demonstrates little or no understanding of the key issues and risks; fails to apply the law to the facts to reach reasonable conclusions • The candidate does not recognise ethical issues or exercise effective judgement in addressing them in accordance with the SRA Principles and rules of professional conduct

PERFORMANCE INDICATORS FOR SQE2
LEGAL RESEARCH ASSESSMENT CRITERIA

Skills	Indicators demonstrating competence	Indicators that do not demonstrate competence

Identify and use relevant sources and information	• The candidate selects relevant information about the legal issue, or the client's problem, from the primary and/or secondary sources provided, eg
	  o the candidate identifies relevant legislation/cases and/or legal explanations/ commentary in a practitioner's text, or legal encyclopaedia
	  o the candidate extracts relevant material, such as particular provision(s) from a statute, or legal rule(s) from the Civil Procedure Rules
	• The candidate uses their findings to substantiate/ support their answer to the question(s) asked
		• The candidate selects only irrelevant information from the primary and/or secondary sources provided
		• The candidate selects insufficient relevant information from the primary and/or secondary sources provided
		• The candidate is unable to distinguish between information that is relevant to the legal issue or the client's problem, and information that is irrelevant, eg the candidate's answer contains information drawn from all sources regardless of relevance, or from a number of irrelevant sources
		• The candidate does not use their findings to substantiate/ support the answer to the question(s) asked

Provide advice that is client-focused and addresses the client's problem	• The candidate demonstrates an understanding of the client's problem from the client's perspective, eg the candidate addresses the client's legal problem, any relevant commercial considerations and/or the client's priorities, objectives and constraints	• The candidate does not understand the problem from the client's perspective, eg they focus on irrelevant issues/provide advice that does not take into account the client's priorities, objectives or constraints, or is inappropriate for the client's situation
Use clear, precise, concise and acceptable language	• The candidate uses understandable and simple language to convey facts and information effectively • The candidate uses correct legal terminology where necessary	• The reader struggles to understand the candidate's use of language; the answer lacks clarity and/or is poorly expressed • The reader's understanding is adversely affected by the density or brevity of the answer • The candidate uses unnecessary or confusing technical terms/legal jargon

Law	Indicators demonstrating competence	Indicators that do not demonstrate competence
Apply the law correctly to the client's situation	• The candidate identifies the relevant legal principles and applies them correctly to the facts of the client's case	• The candidate does not identify and apply the correct legal principles to the facts of the client's case • The candidate identifies the correct legal principles but misapplies them to the client's case
Apply the law comprehensively to the client's situation, identifying any ethical and professional conduct issues and exercising judgement to resolve them honestly and with integrity	• The candidate's legal analysis is sufficiently detailed in the context of the facts of the case, eg the candidate draws on multiple sources of information to address the legal issue/client's problem effectively • Where relevant, the candidate recognises ethical issues and exercises effective judgement in addressing them in accordance with the SRA Principles and rules of professional conduct	• The candidate's legal analysis is not sufficiently detailed in the context of the facts of the client's case • The candidate does not recognise ethical issues or exercise effective judgement in addressing them in accordance with the SRA Principles and rules of professional conduct

PERFORMANCE INDICATORS FOR SQE2
LEGAL WRITING ASSESSMENT CRITERIA

Skills	Indicators demonstrating competence	Indicators that do not demonstrate competence
Include relevant facts	• The candidate refers to and/or addresses the salient facts provided in their instructions. Salient facts could include facts that are important in ensuring the client's needs/objectives are met, or relevant to legal advice	• The candidate includes many facts in their answer that have no bearing on their legal advice
Use a logical structure	• The candidate's presentation of information is well organised, set out clearly and easy to follow • The reader is able to understand the candidate's answer without difficulty	• The candidate's presentation of information is confused and rambling • The reader is unable to follow or understand the candidate's answer
Advice/content is client- and recipient-focused	• The candidate demonstrates an understanding of the client's circumstances including their needs, objectives and priorities • The candidate, where relevant and appropriate, explores options and advises on strategies and solutions • The candidate takes into account who the client is; recognises the key issues in the case and considers any risks • Where appropriate, the candidate imparts any difficult or unwelcome news clearly and sensitively	• The candidate does not understand the client's perspective, eg they focus on irrelevant issues/provide extraneous advice/fail to advise on relevant options, strategies and solutions • The candidate fails to take into account who the client is and does not recognise the key issues in the case or consider any risks • The candidate lacks empathy or sensitivity if imparting difficult or unwelcome news
Use clear, precise, concise and acceptable language that is appropriate to the recipient	• The reader understands the candidate's use of language and clarity of expression • The candidate's language is appropriate to the recipient and the situation • The candidate avoids unnecessary technical terms/legal jargon • The candidate uses formalities appropriate to the context and purpose of the communication	• The reader struggles to understand the candidate's use of language; the answer lacks clarity and/or is poorly expressed • The reader's understanding is adversely affected by the density or brevity of the answer • The candidate uses language that is not appropriate to the recipient and/or the situation, eg the candidate adopts an essay-style approach • The candidate uses unnecessary or confusing technical terms/legal jargon

Law	Indicators demonstrating competence	Indicators that do not demonstrate competence
Apply the law correctly to the client's situation	• The candidate identifies the correct legal principles and applies them correctly to the facts of the case	• The candidate does not identify the correct legal principles • The candidate does not apply the legal principles correctly to the client's situation
Apply the law comprehensively to the client's situation, identifying any ethical and professional conduct issues and exercising judgement to resolve them honestly and with integrity	• The candidate's writing is of sufficient detail in the context of the client's situation and the relevant factual and legal issues • Where relevant, the candidate recognises ethical issues and exercises effective judgement in addressing them in accordance with the SRA Principles and rules of professional conduct	• The candidate's writing is not sufficiently detailed in the context of the client's situation and the relevant factual and legal issues • The candidate does not recognise ethical issues or exercise effective judgement in addressing them in accordance with the SRA Principles and rules of professional conduct

PERFORMANCE INDICATORS FOR SQE2
LEGAL DRAFTING ASSESSMENT CRITERIA

Skills	Indicators demonstrating competence	Indicators that do not demonstrate competence
Use clear, precise, concise and acceptable language	• The candidate uses understandable and simple language to convey facts and information effectively • The candidate uses words and phrases that are suitably formal for the document being drafted • The candidate uses correct legal terminology where necessary • The document uses as few words as possible without compromising the quality of the answer	• The candidate's answer is consistently wordy, repetitive or confusing and cannot be easily understood • The meaning of the document cannot be ascertained because it contains few words • The candidate uses inappropriate language, eg the language is too informal or casual • The candidate uses unnecessary technical terms/ legal jargon throughout
Structure the document appropriately and logically	• The candidate presents facts and information in a methodical way, eg the focus, flow and direction of each paragraph is clear and appropriate signposts are used to guide the reader through the document • The way in which the candidate sets out the contents of the document achieve its purpose	• The candidate's arrangement of facts or information is disjointed or confusing, eg the paragraphing or sequencing of information is illogical • The way in which the candidate sets out the contents of the document does not achieve its purpose
Law	Indicators demonstrating competence	Indicators that do not demonstrate competence
Draft a document that is legally correct	• The candidate identifies the correct legal principles in accordance with the SQE2 assessment specification and applies them correctly in their drafting • The candidate's drafting is legally effective, eg the document contains all key information or the names of relevant parties	• The candidate does not identify the correct legal principles • The candidate does not apply the legal principles correctly in their drafting • The candidate's drafting is not legally effective
Draft a document that is legally comprehensive, identifying any ethical and professional conduct issues and exercising judgement to resolve them honestly and with integrity	• The candidate's drafting is sufficiently detailed in the context of the client's situation and the relevant factual and legal issues • Where relevant, the candidate recognises ethical issues and exercises effective judgement in addressing them in accordance with the SRA Principles and rules of professional conduct	• The candidate's drafting is not sufficiently detailed in the context of the client's situation and the relevant factual and legal issues • The candidate does not recognise ethical issues or exercise effective judgement in addressing them in accordance with the SRA Principles and rules of professional conduct

www.ingramcontent.com/pod-product-compliance
Lightning Source LLC
Chambersburg PA
CBHW082106210326
41599CB00033B/6602